𝕬 𝕿𝖆𝖑𝖊𝖘 𝕱𝖗𝖔𝖒 𝕿𝖍𝖊 𝕭𝖆𝖈𝖐 𝕾𝖎𝖉𝖊 𝕻𝖗𝖊𝖘𝖊𝖓𝖙𝖆𝖙𝖎𝖔𝖓

𝕮𝖍𝖆𝖗𝖑𝖊𝖘 𝕯𝖎𝖈𝖐𝖊𝖓𝖘'𝖘

𝕬 𝕮𝖍𝖗𝖎𝖘𝖙𝖒𝖆𝖘 𝕮𝖆𝖗𝖔𝖑

Retold by

Anthony Lund

First published in Great Britain in 2007 by
Back Side Books

A catalogue record for this book is available from the British Library.

ISBN : 978-0-9556824-0-7
Limited First Edition Hardback

Typeset by me. Less people to pay.

Printed and bound by
A Company.

A Tales From The Back Side Presentation

A Christmas Carol

Retold by

Anthony Lund

Backside Books

Durham

For Spike & Ronnie,
without whom this book may never
have come about.

Stave I

Marley's Spirit

Marley was dead.

This is a thoroughly uplifting start to any story I'm sure you will agree, although it should be noted that if Marley were not dead from the outset then he would have to die sometime around now or we would not be able to have a tale at all. On the whole it is better to begin with someone dead than having to find a suitably macabre, clever and visually pleasing way to pop them off. This is Dickens not Agatha Christie!

So anyway, Marley was definitely deceased and living it up somewhere on the south coast of heaven, getting a nice tan from an updraft from hell.

In the world of the living, situated near Chessington World of Adventures, you would be mistaken for thinking Marley was still alive. His name was there clear to see next to that of Ebenezer Scrooge outside their business premises. It would have taken only a few minutes to paint over Marley's name, but Scrooge had never been fond of decorating – he preferred debt collecting.

𝕬 Christmas Carol - Retold

Scrooge and Marley had been business associates for many years. They had been somewhat married to each other in their misery-making. Neither man had come close to having a meaningful relationship with a female other than of a business nature and it was clear to most that the partners were obviously a pair of whoopsies.

That was in the past, of course. Marley was now, without room for doubt to poke a pinkie through, dead; the usual outcome for someone whose heart no longer beat and whose body had been buried for seven years. Scrooge had overseen the funeral and aided the filling in of the grave just for his own peace of mind. He had applied for Marley's life insurance and wanted no last minute hitches.

It is at this point in our story that we should remind ourselves of one thing; Marley was definitely dead. He was passed over, stone-cold croaked, the rabbit on the tyre, the lamb in the abattoir, ding dong the partner's dead...well you get the idea. It is just to say that Marley was, positively and terminally, dead and buried.

The seven years since Marley's demise had not been kind to Scrooge. He aged gracelessly, had no bingo wins and occasionally suffered incontinence. In short, shit happened. That had not prevented Scrooge enjoying his daily routine every day.

Scrooge liked to think he coined the phrase, "Be a bastard all day, lots of work and no play." The Mars Company had declined to use it as their slogan.   To live by his motto,

Anthony Lund

Scrooge packed his time with many hours of penny pinching, moaning, beating the living shit out of his one member of staff and generally having a merry old time.

He was a rough-skinned hand at the potter's wheel and he would never admit that his favourite film was *Ghost*. Scrooge was every bit the stubborn old goat he was made out to be both inside and out. His nose could be mistaken for a barbeque skewer, so was it pointed and sharp, while his eyes were red rimmed and his lips had a blue tinge. Some would think he had mixed up his eye shadow and lipstick again.

Scrooge was not the type of person to be stopped in the street by anyone, only by no one. People did not feel inclined to ask of his welfare, passing drivers did not feel inclined to tip their hats and dogs showed their appreciation of him by shitting on his shoes. He subsequently showed his appreciation by reinserting the turd where it came from with the aid of his toe.

When Scrooge walked by, tramps leaped into dustbins, children under the age of sixteen hid in their mother's knickers, boys over sixteen hid in their girlfriend's knickers instead – randy buggers will use any excuse – and guide-dogs jumped off bridges to escape him with unfortunate consequences for their owners.

Not that this bothered Scrooge. It made it easier to get through the crowds in Tesco and meant there was always a free checkout for him.

On a particularly cold Christmas Eve in Scrooge's Counting House, two pieces of coal burned slowly in the fireplace giving off the heat of an ant fart. A large bucket of coal stood beside the hearth but Scrooge refused to burn any more than was strictly necessary to prevent his blood freezing in his veins. A thermometer next to the fireplace was constantly speckled with frost, and occasionally a lost penguin would stray into the office mistaking it for the Arctic Circle. Scrooge charged them a transit fee and sent them on their way.

This day, Scrooge's gaze had fallen on the street outside a number of times. He filed a compensation claim against the council and forced them to repave the road.

Fog rolled in from the sea, drunk on pirate's rum and cursing like a sailor. It was virtually impossible to see from one side of the street to the other, and only the dim glow of window candles signalled that there was anything there at all. They also signalled that all was well, dinner was on the table and a flight from New York was cleared for landing.

Inside the Counting House, Scrooge was counting out his money. Bob Cratchit, Scrooge's one employee, was in toilet blowing his nose which had been runny. I could tell you what a maid was doing in the back alley with a blackbird but it would lead to this book being banned in the UK, although I'm sure it would have no such trouble in America.

It was not unfair to say that Scrooge was as tight as a frog's fanny. Trying to get his lottery syndicate money on a Friday was a torturous process that lasted until the following Thursday and a resolution could only ever be agreed by the introduction of

Anthony Lund

a chainsaw and pliers. He never put money into any birthday collections, didn't give money to charity and occasionally turned over his toilet paper to use the other side at a later date.

Scrooge's unfortunate employee, Bob, appeared to be a little weed of a man who found it hard to stand up against a wall. In this instance looks were not deceptive. To Scrooge he was the perfect employee a tight-fisted old bullying goat could wish for.

Cratchit worked tirelessly every day, wrapped in six shirts, two duffel coats, a king-sized duvet and a body warmer, and quite frankly always felt like he was being pissed on from a great height by some monstrous bird with a bladder the size of a dolphin tank. He spent his days in a small room, being constantly watched by Scrooge as hour after hour he copied letters and scrawled entries in ledgers. If the fire smouldering in Scrooge's part of the office was barely adequate then the one provided for Cratchit appeared to be a campfire made by Tom Thumb. Most times it was easier getting heat from his desk candle, although not as easy as burning himself on it, which he did frequently.

The only time Bob had anything to smile about was when he was finally allowed to go home at night and on the few occasions Scrooge received visitors. Seeing someone come into the Counting House with a cheery smile on their face, and leave with their lips trailing in the dirt was always a sight to raise the spirits. Very appropriate.

The arrival of Scrooge's nephew on Christmas Eve was one such occasion. Unlike Scrooge, the other members of his family were hyperactive balls of goodwill and fluff, and his nephew was so unwittingly bright and happy that he had once made a hyena feel inadequate. Of course the blazing joy that erupted from his nephew's every pore had the same effect on Scrooge as a jelly baby thrown at the Great Wall of China.

"Merry Christmas, Uncle!" Scrooge's nephew bellowed, his breath turning to snow inside the Counting House. He stopped to build a snowman out of it.

Scrooge threw his nephew a look of contempt, then reeled it back in to reuse later in the conversation.

"Bah! Bonbons!" Scrooge snapped.

"Shouldn't that be Humbug, Uncle?" his nephew asked.

"Yes, it should but they copyrighted "Bah! Humbug!" and I don't intend to pay to use it!"

"Don't be like that, Uncle. It's Christmas!"

"Really? I thought it was Summer Solstice! I must be going senile."

"I doubt that will happen, Uncle. You don't give anything away so you wouldn't let your mind go without charging it some kind of fee."

Scrooge thought about this for a moment. His mind turned to thoughts of tax, but then he remembered he was not the Sheriff of Nottingham and returned to his paperwork.

"Can I use two pieces of coal for the eyes, Uncle?" Scrooge's nephew asked, patting the last of the snowman's head in place.

Anthony Lund

"Only if you pay for them."

"How much?"

Scrooge quickly counted on his fingers. There were ten of them. Someone had stolen his thumbs and cunningly replaced them with spare fingers. Scrooge bit one of them. They were chocolate fingers. He pulled them off to have later with his tea.

"Fifty pounds," Scrooge said finally.

"For two pieces of coal?" his nephew exclaimed.

"No, as a reward for the person who finds my thumbs!"

The room suddenly went dark. The window was full of faces.

"I wasn't being serious," Scrooge shouted.

Light returned to the room. It had a tan and was wearing a sombrero.

"You're a bit of a grouch, aren't you Uncle?"

"You're like the Laughing Fucking Policeman. What's your excuse?"

"I'm high on Christmas spirit!" Scrooge's nephew bellowed, blowing off the snowman's head.

"Can't you check into rehab?"

"I really can't say I would want to. Anyway, don't you want to know why I'm here, Uncle?"

"No."

"Well I'm here to invite you to Christmas Lunch."

"I said I didn't want to know."

"If you didn't know what I was going to say then how could you reject the offer?"

Scrooge looked up. "This is true. I reject your offer."

"You do the same thing every year, Uncle."

"Then that just shows how thick you are to keep asking me, doesn't it?"

"Not at all, Uncle. It means that we've bought too much food again and are trying to get as many people as possible round to eat it. We'll still be eating turkey sandwiches at Easter if not."

"Well I won't be one of your guests," Scrooge grumbled. "Besides I've seen your wife's cooking. It always reminds me of cheery, family gatherings."

"Uncle, that was almost complimentary. Are you feeling well?"

"You didn't let me finish. I was going to say cheery, family gatherings usually attended by cannibals. You're never quite sure what it is you're eating. Perhaps if there wasn't always a thick layer of charcoal on everything it would be better."

"Ah. That sounds more like you, Uncle. So I definitely can't tempt you then?"

"A whole host of demons from beyond the grave couldn't drag me there. They'd have to bring me in a wheelbarrow."

"What if I send the mother-in-law round?" Scrooge's nephew enquired.

"I'll send her back square."

Anthony Lund

Scrooge's nephew hovered around the desk like a boomerang in human form until Scrooge pleasantly asked him to fuck off.

"Will you pleasantly fuck off, nephew? And take that holly wreath with you!"

"But I brought it for your office, Uncle. To brighten the place up!"

"Can't you take a hint? I don't want your Christmas cheer, or your Christmas Dinner, or your holly wreath! You deal with Christmas in your way and I'll deal with it with rat poison. It's not as though it has done any good for anyone."

"Maybe I have not become richer for it, but I consider that my life has. I feel love and joy and Christmas cheer that you don't seem to want. I share my Christmas with as many people as I can whether they are rich or poor. Ok, it is mainly to help get rid of that bloody turkey but that is beside the point. What I am saying, Uncle, is that while you sit here with your piles of cold money, I can spend Christmas in the warmth of my family where any family man should be!"

A round of applause burst into the room. It carried a placard bearing the words, "Free Speech For All."

Scrooge shot it dead then turned to Bob Cratchit. "One more clap from you and you'll be looking for a new job."

Bob was about to say he had never had the clap, but thought better of it and returned to his work.

A Christmas Carol - Retold

"As for you," Scrooge said to his nephew. "You are very good at rallying the brainless. Have you considered a career in Parliament?"

"Unfortunately, Uncle, I would be no use there. I'm not a good liar."

"Neither are most of the buggers in there but that doesn't stop them trying."

"So I really can't convince you to come around tomorrow, Uncle?"

Scrooge vaulted over the desk with the agility of a champion hurdler, sending coins scattering everywhere like pennies from heaven, picked up the wreath and forced it over his nephew's head. He opened the door, spun his nephew around and kicked him out into the street.

"I'm sure you will agree that actions speak louder than words, nephew. And so we are perfectly clear, to your Christmas I say, Bah! Sherbet Lemons!"

"Hpy Nw Yrr, Ncle," his nephew said through a mouthful of pavement and holly wreath.

Scrooge slammed the door so hard that all of the coins in the Counting House jumped to attention and restacked themselves on his desk.

As he walked back to his desk a knock came at the door. There was a hand on the other end of it.

Scrooge opened the door to reveal the knocker. It was brass and still attached to the wood. Scrooge was glad to see

18

Anthony Lund

this still in place, but less happy to be faced with two people who looked very much like charity collectors.

"Yes?" Scrooge asked bluntly.

The two men stood in stunned silence for a moment before one of them spoke.

"Eiiiieeoooooo," he said.

"I must apologise for my colleague," said the other. "He is easily tongue-tied. Excuse me while I undo the knot. We won't be a moment."

Scrooge tapped his foot while he waited then pulled a pint of lager from it.

A moment later the second man spoke again.

"Am I talking to Mr Scrooge or Mr Marley?" he asked.

"Marley has been dead for seven years," Scrooge said.

"So you must be Mr Scrooge?"

"You're bright, aren't you? Have this dunce cap."

"Oh, well, thank you."

"And now I'll have it back."

The man handed over the hat with a look of genuine sorrow. He really wasn't that bright, certainly no more than about 20 watts.

"You want money from me, don't you?" Scrooge said.

"Erm, what makes you think that, Sir?" the first man said.

"You look suspiciously like charity collectors to me. And you're carrying a box that says "Please give generously" on it. It's something of a giveaway."

19

"Ah. Yes. Not very subtle is it? Well, would you like to give to the Suspicious Charity? We aim to help all those unfortunate bad eggs who can't fund their own lurking and world domination plans."

"It's different from the usual do-gooders I suppose," Scrooge said thoughtfully.

"We like to think these people are often victimised against and need our support."

"Have you had any success?"

"Moderate. A man who needed some face reconstruction was one of our more recent beneficiaries. He had a bad experience with a man in a bat costume and ended up in a vat of acid. Nasty business. And if it isn't Fathers for Justice causing them problems, there's a particularly irritating man called Bond who has a habit of blowing them up before their plans take off."

"Tragic," Scrooge said. "Should these people not be in prisons with the poor? I hear they get air conditioning these days."

"I believe they do, Sir. It sometimes seems that crime does pay."

"Is it a good wage, do you know?"

"I think it depends on the crime, Mr Scrooge."

"Ah, a pay on performance business."

"Precisely," the first gentleman said with a spreading smile. "Now the only thing left for me to ask is how much are you going to give us?"

Anthony Lund

"Fuck all," Scrooge replied.

"How many fuck alls would that be?"

"I'm sorely tempted to let you keep the dunce cap. At least I would know it had gone to a good home. I wish to thank you fine, porky, well-fed gentlemen for your bit of bad cheer and it is nice to know there are people out there who are looking to bring misery to others by funding the villains of the world. Unfortunately, I am too busy funding my own misery factory to contribute. So all I have to say to you is good day."

Scrooge slammed the door. From the other side he heard a short series of scratching sounds, a tinkle of metal and footsteps running down the street. He opened the door to find the knocker had been stolen. Hanging out of the door, he saw the shapes of the two thieving charity collectors trotting down the road.

"Bastards!" he shouted. "I hate people fiddling with my knockers."

"I know just how you feel, darling," said a passing madam.

Scrooge looked momentarily puzzled then a light burst into his head like a match in a gunpowder store. "Bah! Pear drops!"

Scrooge slammed the door and returned to his desk.

Bob Cratchit had not moved during the whole episode. He found it difficult to do much of anything while wearing half his wardrobe and his earlier applause had knackered him.

A Christmas Carol - Retold

Nonetheless he had been thoroughly entertained to see someone other than himself being bullied by Scrooge. It made his day worthwhile, which was just as well as his wage did not warrant getting out of bed on a morning.

Outside a thicker fog had come in from the sea. It brought a haul of cod and a basket full of crabs. Somewhere in the middle of town the church bell chimed every quarter of the hour. By eight o'clock at night it was becoming a fucking nuisance.

As the hour drew on, it became yet colder. The number of people out in the streets grew fewer, and those who remained out had either no home or no sense. One such person paused by Scrooge's establishment on his way to warm himself in the freezer section of Tesco. He bent to the letter box and began to sing his favourite Christmas song.

"My grandma got flattened by a drunken reindeer..."

The singing halted when the caroller felt something cold and metallic emerge from the letterbox and come to rest on his tongue.

"Go ahead, punk," Scrooge said from inside. "Make my Christmas."

The caroller wisely decided to keep his brain intact and fled. Inside, Scrooge dropped the gun into his drawer and locked it. Bob Cratchit was pulling his coat on. From a distance he bore a passing resemblance to the Michelin Man.

Anthony Lund

"I guess you won't want to come into work tomorrow?" Scrooge asked.

"Well it is Christmas Day, Mr Scrooge."

"So it is. I'd completely forgotten. That wonderful day when I pay you a full day's wage and you do fuck all for me."

"That's right, Mr Scrooge. I'll make up for it when I come back the next day though."

"Damn right you will, Cratchit, or I'll be using your head to poke the fire."

Bob and Scrooge both turned to the fireplace. The piece of coal went out. Scrooge watched it leave in a taxi with a stone and a twig.

"Or I'll find some other way to punish you," Scrooge said lamely. "You'd better be in here early on Thursday."

"That would be Boxing Day."

"I'll be boxing you if you aren't early."

"Ok. Merry Christmas, Mr Scrooge."

"Will you piss off?"

Bob hurried out of the door and almost strangled himself when his scarf caught on the door handle. He quickly untangled himself and rushed off down the street towards home and his family. Scrooge followed soon after, locking the property for the night.

Scrooge stopped into The Pig's Head Tavern, the same grubby little establishment he had called in every night of his working life. He ate a small meal, drank a small drink, had a small piss and paid in small change. As always he made his way home using small steps for continuity, and a long time later he arrived at his front door.

Scrooge lived in a house that had been owned by his former partner. It was not exactly the House of Fun, but Scrooge did make money on the side renting it to horror movie makers. The large yard outside the building was unlit at night, and even though Scrooge knew the yard like the back of his hand, he had gone arse over tit on a number of occasions.

As he stood on the doorstep, fog played around Scrooge's ankles.

"Piss off," he snapped. "That tickles."

He put the key in the lock and turned it.

"Scrooooooge," it said.

Scrooge looked at the lock. It usually made a creaking sound.

He turned the key again.

"Scrooooooge," the sound came again. This time he realised it was a pitiful voice.

Scrooge spun around with the finesse of a ballet champion, and raised his cane ready to hospitalise someone. There was no one there. Turning back to the door, Scrooge noticed something strange about this door-knocker. Those bloody charity workers had stolen it and replaced it with a hockey mask. He made a mental note to hunt them down in the morning.

Anthony Lund

"Bah! Jelly Babies!" Scrooge muttered as he opened the door and stepped inside.

Scrooge lit a candle which flared unexpectedly and singed his eyebrows. He fastened the door and made his way up the stairs to his residence. The staircase was broader than an elephant's arse and Scrooge's candle could barely light the next step. When he finally made it to the landing, he had stumbled twice, tripped over three times and burnt his hand with candle wax.

Upstairs he walked through his rooms; sitting room, bedroom, toilet. All of them were still there. Everything appeared to be normal. The rooms were empty, his toilet paper was still drying on the radiator, his morning leftovers were still on the table ready for in the morning and his fridge was still empty.

Satisfied, Scrooge locked his door, strung his crossbow to the handle and removed its safety catch. No one was getting inside with both eyes intact.

He poured himself a drink and slouched into his chair. His copy of Miser Monthly was just out of reach and he refused to exert himself to reach out for it. Instead he just sat and waited for nothing to happen.

He was not disappointed – nothing happened.

Then Scrooge heard a tinkle. He checked to make sure he had not done it in his pants. He realised it was an old bell above the fireplace. This was no time to have a fire drill in the building. Suddenly another bell began to toll. A third followed, and another until all the bells in the building seemed to swinging. Scrooge held his crotch as it began to twitch.

"What the hell is this about?" Scrooge yelled over the cacophony.

The room fell silent. Somewhere below him there came the thump of a heavy door being thrown open, then the sound of it swinging closed and finally a muffled voice saying, "Oww. That was my nose."

Scrooge listened as further thumps and bumps and frequent bursts of profanity came from below. The sound of heavy, lumbering footsteps approached, first up the stairs before plodding along the landing outside Scrooge's door.

Remaining still in his chair, Scrooge heard what sounded like a lumberjack chopping logs. Wood splintered, and Scrooge was certain someone was chopping down a door with an axe.

From somewhere on the landing, a little beyond Scrooge's door the echoes of destruction ceased and a voice could clearly be heard to say, "Here's Jacob! Oh fuck, not again. I get the wrong one every time!"

The clock on Scrooge's mantelpiece chimed twelve. Scrooge realised something wasn't right. He looked around the room. Everything seemed ok. There was nothing out of place he could see. His thumbs were still missing, but he had been living with that all day. All of a sudden he realised what was wrong. His trousers had fallen down.

Anthony Lund

Scrooge bent over to pull up his pants just as a large machete split the chair behind him. Scrooge jumped up, tripped over his trousers and fell flat on his face.

Over the top of the chair, a large shape wearing a hockey mask struggled to pull the machete free. Scrooge was slightly unnerved.

"Who the fuck are you?" he asked, a quite plausible question to ask someone who has just tried to lop your head off.

"Ask me who the fuck I was?"

"I'll kick your arse unless you tell me."

"Don't you recognise me, Scrooge?" the mask asked.

"Were you in the keeper in the Durham Wasps vs Newcastle Vipers match the other week?"

"No, I've never played Ice Hockey. I have trouble with my balance, as you should know."

"I haven't hit you with my cane before, have I?" Scrooge asked.

"No." said the mask.

In a blur of naked leg, loose trousers and flying stick, Scrooge launched into a frenzied cane attack that left the mask wearer in a heap on the floor.

"Well I have now." Scrooge said, hoiking up his trousers and giving the groaning heap a final dig in the ribs.

"Scrooge, it's me," the heap wheezed. "Jacob Marley."

Scrooge looked momentarily puzzled. "Why are you dressed like a homicidal sportsman?"

27

"I got sick of the chains and having that scarf wrapped around my jaw. Thought it was time for a change and this was all I could get my hands on."

"Oh," was all Scrooge could think to say. "I thought you were dead. I signed to say you were anyway. And I got the life insurance."

Something that looked like pound signs flashed in Scrooge's eyes. He quickly pulled them out and tucked them in his pocket then recommenced thrashing the death out of his former partner.

"I'm not going to give the life insurance money back!"

"Scrooge. I am dead." Marley managed to say between cane blows. "You've been watching too much of *The Matrix*!"

Scrooge stepped back. "Oh, sorry. Just making sure."

Marley stood up and dusted himself down. His face fell off.

"Shit," his mouth said from the floor. "I hate it when that happens."

"It's not amazingly appetising from where I'm standing either," Scrooge commented.

Marley picked up his face and slapped it back into place.

"Can you sit down?" Scrooge asked the shade.

"Have you tried to sit down dressed like this?"

"No I can't say I have. How do I know you're real?"

Marley put a hand to his head. "I could get the machete out again."

Anthony Lund

"No, it's fine," Scrooge said quickly. "I believe you're real, or maybe you're really just in my imagination. Perhaps The Pig's Head used out of date gravy on my meal tonight, or someone slipped something in my drink. To you I say just one thing. Bah! Aniseed Balls!"

Suddenly Marley's Ghost opened his mouth to release an unearthly sound that rattled the windows in their frames and caused Scrooge to hold onto his chair as a great, raging wind whipped around him. After a few seconds the wind died and Scrooge dropped to the floor with a thud.

"Sorry," Marley said, patting his chest. "It must have been something I ate."

"It smells of garlic," Scrooge said, wrinkling his nose. "No more! Please, no more! Just tell me why you are here and be gone."

"I'm here to warn you to change your ways."

"And you think trying to slice my head open with a machete and burping in my face will help achieve your goal?"

Marley shrugged. "You were always hard to get through to. I thought a different approach might work better."

Scrooge began to wonder if he had underestimated his partner all those years. Although Marley had always seemed to be the more reasonable of the two, Scrooge now saw that perhaps he did have something of a psychotic streak running through him. Such a shame he was dead and couldn't be used to demand money with menaces...or maybe he could. Hauntings were all the rage these days.

"Are you sure you don't want to sit down?" Scrooge asked. "You're rather intimidating standing up."

"No."

"Do you want a drink?"

"Yes."

"Good you can get me one while you're there," Scrooge said, picking himself up off the floor. "I thought ghosts were meant to carry their chains with them. You know, the ones they have gathered from the wrongdoings of their lives."

"You talk shit sometimes, Scrooge. They went casual years ago. No more regulation uniforms. It just really irritates me that I couldn't get the costume I really wanted."

"What was that?"

"The Ballerina one. Goddamned Ghengis Khan beat me to it."

Scrooge felt a sudden need to change the subject.

"So what exactly are you warning me about?"

"Oh yes, I almost forgot in all the excitement. I came to warn you that you will be haunted by three Spirits."

"You're not making me feel any happier," Scrooge said sourly.

"Do I look like a clown?"

"No. Who got that costume?"

"The shade of Charlie Chaplin."

Anthony Lund

"Figures," Scrooge said.

"As I was saying, you will be visited by these Spirits whether it pleases you or not. They've already been booked and you really don't want to know what their cancellation rates are. They go by the names of Gin, Vodka and Whiskey."

"Catchy," Scrooge commented.

"They do tend to linger with you the morning after. You will receive the first tomorrow night at the chime of one."

"I didn't know Royal Mail did night deliveries."

"He is coming special delivery from the other side."

"All the way from Australia. He'll be tired."

"Expect the next Spirit the same time the next night, and the last at the stroke of twelve the night after that. "

Scrooge looked aghast. "Don't any of them sleep? I'll be knackered by the time they're done. Can't they just all come together? We could play poker or something."

"Do you want the chance of redemption or not?"

"I'm beginning to wonder."

"Be prepared, Scrooge. The Spirits will make you see things differently."

"I can handle my spirits, Marley."

"We'll see. Now it is time for me to go."

"Where will you go now?" Scrooge asked. "Do you have an apartment nearby?"

"Don't be a dick, Scrooge."

A Christmas Carol - Retold

Marley backed away towards the window as he talked. Scrooge raised his hand to speak.

"Scrooge, I don't want you to plead with me. Save that for the others, I can't be bothered."

"No I was just going to say–"

"Save it. I'm really not one for the whole "spare me please from these ghosts" routine. I just want to be on my waaaaaaaaa–"

A thump from below cut off Marley's surprised yell. Scrooge walked over to the window. From down in the street he could hear a series of grunts and moans that sounded like someone being trampled on by a great crowd of people. He looked out into the street.

Marley was lying on his back being trampled on by a great crowd of people. Scrooge squinted to try and find some faces in the crowd. There were plenty of them but they seemed to be strangely detached from the bodies they belonged to. Every single one of them was dead. They were ghosts like Marley, although Marley was somewhat worse for wear under their spectral feet.

Scrooge stepped back from the window. He could surely not have just seen what he thought he had. One of the ghosts had been naked!

"I'll send you an invoice for my time in the next few days," came Marley's voice from the street.

Scrooge stuck his head out of the window again.

Anthony Lund

"What?!" Scrooge yelled but Marley had already vanished along with the other spirits. "Bastard!"

Scrooge closed his window against the draft. Maybe he had imagined the whole thing. On turning around he was drawn to the large chunk missing from his chair.

No, he had not imagined it. There was only one thing for it – drastic action was required. He would have to wait until one o'clock tomorrow morning to see if Marley's warning proved true.

Scrooge retired to bed and fell into a deep, dark sleep. Soon he was snoring to wake the dead and drooling like a pervert at an Ann Summers party.

And in the silence of the room, wrapped in the arms of sleep, Scrooge muttered into his pillow.

"Bah! Cola Cubes!"

Stave II

Gin – A Spirit Past The Sweet Shop

Scrooge awakened in darkness.

Insomnia was a bitch. He could barely have slumbered more than an hour, so dark was the room about him.

Suddenly he heard something outside. It was the chiming of the church clock. Counting the bongs, Scrooge came to grand total of twelve.

Scrooge nodded with satisfaction, then rolled over and closed his eyes.

Then opened them again in a movement so quick they resembled a pair of released roll blinds.

It couldn't be twelve o'clock. He hadn't gone to bed until almost one, and no way could he have slept almost twenty four hours. There was only one explanation – the sun had burned out and the ice age had arrived!

Scrooge threw back his covers and instantly felt the cold hugging him. He beat it with his stick until it let go and retreated into a corner.

He hurried to the window and pressed his face to the glass like a hungry kid outside an all-you-can-eat buffet. The frost on the inside of the window stuck to his lips.

"Mah! 'Ollipops!"

He tugged his head back until his lips stretched before him like a pair of skis. Suddenly there came the sound of two Velcro strips being pulled apart and Scrooge's lips hit him in the face. He collapsed to the floor with a thud and his top lip poked him in the eye.

Picking himself up, Scrooge tied his stretched lips around his forehead to keep them out of the way then returned to the window.

This time he slid it open and stuck his head out into the chilly air. The street was silent and shrouded in fog. It could simply not be midday of Christmas Day.

Scrooge went to pull his head inside. Instead he slammed it against the window which fell shut on his hand.

"Shittingcockarsefucker," Scrooge blurted, inadvertently diving forward and splatting his face against the frosted glass again. "Arrrgghhhh!"

A few minutes passed in chaos then Scrooge returned to bed looking like the mummy. The window looked like the gory set

Anthony Lund

of a horror movie. On the up side, Scrooge had not suffered any further digit loss.

To prevent him dwelling on the continued mystery of his missing thumbs, Scrooge pondered on what could have caused him to sleep through a whole day.

Then he remembered Marley. He also remembered the machete, the garlic burp and the ghost's promise of a bill. Marley had warned him that he would be visited at one o'clock by the first of three Spirits.

It was clear that only drastic action would suffice. Scrooge would sit awake and watch the minutes tick by. It was not going to be the most enthralling evening he had spent, but it would certainly pass the time.

The minutes passed by slowly. Scrooge offered it a scooter to speed it up.

Finally, the hour approached. Scrooge bellowed a countdown.

"Five. Four. Three. Two. One. Aha! Not a single splat of ectoplasm to be seen. There is only one thing I have to say, Marley, and it will be worth every penny! Bah! Hum–"

As the chime of one faded a brilliant light charged into the room wearing knight's armour and riding a white horse. It hit the wall causing minor structural damage.

As Scrooge watched transfixed, the curtains around his bed slowly began to open.

Scrooge leapt forward and pulled them shut again.

Something pulled them open from the other side.

Scrooge yanked them shut.

A white hand poked through the gap in the fabric and twisted Scrooge's right nipple.

"Ya bastard!" Scrooge shouted, letting go of the curtain to tend to his throbbing nipple.

The curtains opened wide and light spilled on the bed.

"If that stains I'll be sending you the cleaning bill," Scrooge grumbled.

Scrooge looked the figure up and down. Then down a bit further, and down further still. He finally found a face about three feet from the floor.

The Spirit had a childish appearance, but also that of an old man. Its hair was the colour of ancient parchment and in need of a wash, but its skin bore no wrinkle and seemed freshly ironed. It was simultaneously aged and youthful to the eye. I know, confusing isn't it?

It wore a dress of white, trimmed with daffodils and pansies, which flowed from its neck to its feet. Then, most peculiar of all, from its head emitted the source of the light in the room – a great shaft of brilliance that showed off the cobwebs and the dust in Scrooge's bedroom. Under its left arm it carried a large candle extinguisher (no prizes in guessing what it used that for), and in its right hand it carried a small paper bag.

"Bah! Jelly Teddies!" Scrooge said, although his heart was not in it.

Anthony Lund

"Cola bottles actually," said the Spirit, holding out the bag. "Want one?"

"I was told never to accept sweets from strangers," Scrooge said.

"How old are you? Grow up!"

"I'm not the short-arse here," Scrooge retorted. "OW!"

Scrooge rubbed his head and looked down at the cola bottle that had just been pelted off his head.

"I thought spirits were supposed to be gentle, lost souls looking for salvation. So far one's tried to crack my head like a coconut and another is stotting hard jellies off my head!"

"We have to get our kicks some way," said the Ghost. "Anyway, I'm Gin, The Ghost of Christmas Past."

"Does that mean you're a rerun? Christmas is always full of reruns these days!"

"Well get used to it cos you're stuck with me for a while, and I'm stuck in your past Christmases. I could think of better things to do with my time."

Scrooge thought of asking what else a ghost stuck in other people's pasts could find to do but thought better of it. He wasn't that interested and had an idea that asking the question would open the floodgates on all the boring times this ghost had spent doing his job. Scrooge had never been one for a sob story and the sooner he could get rid of the ancient kid the better he would feel.

"Are we going to start or just stand here all night?" Scrooge asked.

"Both."

"What?"

Gin clicked his fingers and the room melted around them to reveal an old country road. Scrooge breathed in the country air. It smelled of shit. He glanced down to find a great mound of steaming horse dung in which his right foot was firmly planted.

"You had the whole pissing road and you chose this spot!" Scrooge complained, trying to scrape his foot clean on the rough surface.

"Trust me," said the Spirit. "That's the least of your worries. Do you recognise it?"

"It's horse shit! Am I meant to look for distinguishing marks?"

"I was referring to this place," Gin said.

"Oh. Erm...yes, yes I do. I was born here. With thumbs I might add."

Scrooge was suddenly overtaken by a thousand lost memories. They mooned at him as they sped by.

"Your lip seems to be trembling," Gin said, then with great amusement, "And you're starting to cry! Haha."

"It's bloody cold," Scrooge said, with little conviction. "I'm cold and the breeze is making my eyes water. Show me what we are here for and get on with it."

Anthony Lund

"Fair enough," Gin said, sucking on a lollipop. "Do you think you can remember how to get to the school from here?"

"Of course I do. I could make it there blindfolded!"

"Good," said Gin. "Put this one on and see how far you get."

Scrooge pulled the blindfold over his eyes and took a step forward straight into the overhanging branch of a tree.

"Ok, maybe we could do it without the blindfold," he mumbled.

Together they walked along the road to the old school of Scrooge's childhood. Scrooge recognised everything that passed by. The gate, the trees, the tramp, the shagging dogs, the blonde on her knees and the dark haired man who was...

"Hey! I don't remember them!"

...helping her pick up the money she had dropped.

"Oh, sorry. Continue."

Crowds of happy young children played and laughed and yelled. One of them screamed as his friends gave him a wedgie that went all the way up to his chin.

"It's bloody noisy here," Scrooge said to Gin.

"There used to be a remote control somewhere for the volume but I lost it."

"Really?"

"Of course not," Gin said, flicking his lolly stick over his shoulder. "These are images from your past, meant to be seen as they were then. It was noisy then so it's noisy now. Ok?"

Scrooge nodded.

"Good. Now I'm sure you know that the school should be empty for Christmas but when you were there it never was, was it?"

"I never saw anyone when I was there," Scrooge said.

"Obviously those many hours spent studying over Christmas really helped improve your intellect. You were there! How could the place be deserted if there was someone inside?"

"Oh," was the best Scrooge could do.

The school building was still quite a walk away. Its roof poked over the tops of the trees lining the road.

"Hang on," Gin said, stopping Scrooge by tripping him over.

"What was that for?" Scrooge said through a bloodied lip as he lifted his face off the road.

"I wanted to stop you."

"You could have asked!"

"Oh, yeah," Gin pondered. "I never thought of that. Well no harm done."

Scrooge opened his mouth to protest but was silenced as the outdoors melted away around him, revealing behind it a large classroom that he recognised as his own.

"Nice trick," Scrooge said, thinking of all the travelling expenses that could be saved with such a talent.

"I know," Gin said, slurping through a wine gum. "Now, do you recognise anyone here?"

Anthony Lund

Scrooge looked at the room before him. It was empty.

"I think I might know that chair from somewhere," he said.

"Oh, what a comedian thou art. Turn around, div."

Scrooge looked over his shoulder. The room was not empty after all. There was one young man sitting at a desk near the back wall.

"Handsome fellow, isn't he?" Scrooge commented with a distant smile. "With thumbs too."

"Yeah," said the Spirit, looking Scrooge up and down. "Where did it all go wrong?"

"Look you might be a Spirit, but you're still small enough to be taken over my knee."

"They never told me you were that way inclined. Now, don't you see anything unusual about this sight after all we witnessed on the road outside?"

"Should I?"

The Spirit shook his head. "They told me it was going to be like a brick wall. The boy is all alone here. Everyone else is out enjoying the build up to Christmas."

Scrooge looked at the image of his young self. He felt something in his eye.

"Hey, stop poking me!" Scrooge protested.

"Sorry. I just had an urge. Don't you feel a little sad for him? Your young self all alone here? Just like the Caroller who came to your door last night."

Scrooge thought for a moment. "You're right. I should have shot him and put him out of his misery."

"Not quite what I was thinking, but never mind."

Gin produced a fizzy lace from out of the air.

"How about we move on now? There are more past Christmases to see."

The room shimmered around them. Gin stamped his foot and the shimmering stopped.

"Sorry," he said. "I've been meaning to get that fixed for a while now."

He snapped his fingers and the younger Scrooge aged in an instant, turning from a child to a young man.

The room had not changed much. The only real change was that young Scrooge was no longer sitting at his desk; he walked around the room instead. After walking in a circle three times he lost his balance and crashed into a nearby chair.

Scrooge winced, remembering the pain.

"You were quite dumb in your younger days, weren't you?" Gin observed.

Before Scrooge could answer, a door to their left was thrown open. It landed on the other side of the room and a young girl ran in. Scrooge felt something stir in his stomach.

"Please take your hand out of my gut," he told the Spirit. "It's not hygienic."

"Sorry. Just checking I could still pass through things."

Anthony Lund

"And with all these desks and doors and walls you opt to try with my stomach?"

"It was convenient. Do you want to know the stage of digestion you last meal is at?"

"That's disgusting. How did you get this job?"

"I had to go through Hell. It's quite nice there but not somewhere I'd like to stay."

Scrooge was about to comment when Gin gestured for him to watch what was happening around them. Scrooge watched the scene, sensing that he now knew what it was like to have an out of body experience.

The little girl ran up to young Scrooge and threw herself at him. Her outstretched hand caught his windpipe and her trailing foot landed squarely in his nuts.

Scrooge and the Ghost inadvertently tensed.

"Brother, dear bother!" the girl screeched in childish ecstasy. "I've come to take you home!"

"I thought you'd come to put me in hospital," young Scrooge said. "Why would I want to come home?"

"Because I asked dad and he said you could come home and be a man!"

"He just wants more rent money."

"Oh, but there's a pink limo waiting outside and we could have such a gay old time, brother!"

"And I'm not Fred Flintstone!"

47

A Christmas Carol - Retold

The little girl laughed and clapped like a hyperactive sea lion. She grabbed young Scrooge's hand and dragged him along the floor towards the door. She had amazing strength for one so young. The spinach was working wonders.

Young Scrooge's head bounced off the floor and table legs as his freak of a sister hurried out of the room like a deranged husky pulling a sled.

Scrooge could remember every bump of that sleigh ride, and oh what fun it was not to ride.

Out in the hallway a booming voice rang out, and the wind on its tail blew the girl off her feet. She landed on young Scrooge's back and her feet landed his face. He wriggled her toe out of his nostril.

"Someone fetch me Master Scrooge's belongings!" the bulky figure bellowed, causing plaster to fall from the ceiling.

The school Head Master was a very imposing figure, standing ten feet tall and five feet wide. At least that's how it always appeared to Young Scrooge – it was an easy thing to assume when the Head Master constantly bumped his head on doorframes.

"I see you are finally leaving us for once," the Head Master said. "I myself do not approve of the festive period and having my students dancing off down the path yonder like the Riverdance Appreciation Society. I always thought you were made of stronger stuff, Master Scrooge, and I have not been

Anthony Lund

disappointed. I have seen building foundations that are not as steadfast.

"But now you leave with this little hyperactive child. I do not blame you. Refusing to do so would seemingly lose you your arm. Ah, here is your trunk."

A large case, encrusted with muck and cobwebs was dragged along the hallway by a servant. So long had it remained undisturbed that it appeared to be some ancient relic just discovered in an abandoned tomb.

Moments later, the trunk had been loaded into the waiting car, and Young Scrooge and his little sister were on their way to enjoy the merriest of Christmases.

"You don't need to puke do you?" Gin asked as he nibbled at a sugar cane.

"Sorry," Scrooge said. "Was I gagging that loud?"

"Oh nothing that couldn't be heard more than fifty years away. I have to say she was full of joy."

"Yes, she was. It was annoying."

"She died I believe, leaving one son."

Scrooge paused a moment, then said, "That fool that calls himself my nephew. At least everyone knows where he got it from."

Scrooge suddenly realised they were no longer inside the school.

"Where are we now?" Scrooge asked.

"Look over there," Gin said, pointing to a building across the road.

"Dirty Carrie's? Of course! How could I forget? That was where Madame Lucia took me into the back room and gave me an hour of bliss with her great big–"

"I meant the building next to that one, Scrooge," Gin said.

"Oh," Scrooge replied. "Of course! How could I forget? It's old Fezziwig's! This was where I had my first job!"

"Calm down, Scrooge. I'm not insured for you having a coronary."

The Spirit led Scrooge inside. The first person Scrooge saw was a huge man wearing a Welch wig.

"It's the big man himself!" Scrooge exclaimed. "Fezziwig here and alive before me."

Fezziwig sat behind a desk large enough to accommodate the full extended Royal Family, yet he seemed to occupy much of the available space. He finished writing a line in his ledger and went to put his pen behind his ear, inadvertently poking himself in the eye in the process. He looked at his watch. The face of Mickey Mouse looked back at him. He really needed to think about getting something more manly.

"Ebenezer!" Fezziwig called out. "Dick!"

Scrooge's younger self poked his head out of an open door.

"Who're you calling a dick?" Young Scrooge asked.

Anthony Lund

"The other person I employ besides you!"

"It's a bit harsh calling him a dick though."

Fezziwig shook his head in despair as he stood from his desk. "That's his name, Scrooge. Are you sure you're an educated man?"

Dick made an appearance.

"Mr Fezziwig," Young Scrooge said. "Your trousers have fallen down."

Fezziwig quickly pulled them up and tucked himself in. Meanwhile, Dick had joined Scrooge in the room.

"Now boys," Fezziwig said. "It's Christmas Eve! Let's have those shutters up before you can say, "almighty pissup". Let's move all this furniture out of the way too. We want this room empty. Get to it!"

Dick and Young Scrooge took off at 200 miles per hour, creating a wind that blew the cobwebs from the rafters and sent the furniture crashing into the far corner of the large room. A couple of passing beavers leaned in through the window and gathered up the remains of a broken chair and offered a quick "Merry Christmas" before running off to finish their dam.

In mere moments the warehouse had been transformed into a dance hall to rival the Tower Ballroom.

Fezziwig opened up the warehouse doors to usher in the guests.

The crowds rushed in like a stampede of wildebeests, flattening Old Fezziwig to the floor. The chant of "Drink. Drink.

A Christmas Carol - Retold

Food and Drink!" echoed around the hall as the mass of bodies charged towards Dick's bar which had been erected in the corner of the room. There were many recognisable members of the community in the alcohol hunting mob – employees of Fezziwig's, the local policeman, the district nurse, the butcher, the baker, the candlestick maker, the local author, a newspaper reporter, the vicar, the harbourmaster, the fiddle player, a clown, a gorilla-gram, a flasher and a prostitute.

Scrooge's eyes lit up at the sight of this last. "It's Madame Lucia! Oh how I remember her well."

Scrooge felt his groin twitch.

"Get the fuck off, you pervert!" Scrooge snapped at the Ghost.

"You wanted to take me over your knee and you call me the pervert?"

"That was to punish you!"

Gin raised an eyebrow at Scrooge but did not say a word.

"I'm not making this any better, am I?" Scrooge asked.

"Not really," Gin replied. "I could have given you a shovel to save time."

Members of the Fezziwig family were entering the room in the wake of the mass of townsfolk. They paused to peel Old Fezziwig from the wooden floorboards then walked into the centre of the room, grinning like the occupants of an Amsterdam brothel.

Anthony Lund

Or perhaps a client of Madame Lucia and her huge...

"Melons!" Fezziewig bellowed. "Alfred Melons. How is the grocery business?"

Fezziwig made his way through the crowd, greeting everyone and stepping on the toes of many.

In the corner, Fred the fiddle player began to fiddle for the crowd.

"Put it away, you dirty bastard!" a voice heckled.

Fred quickly put it away. A few moments later he had unpacked his fiddle and was playing a lively little tune; so lively that it almost escaped out of the window.

"What are we doing here?" Scrooge asked.

"Well I'm going for a pint!"

"You can't. You're a ghost!"

"You really do like making other people miserable don't you?"

Scrooge shrugged. "I've kind of perfected it over the years."

"Well you need to try and un-perfect it. I'm not here for the good of my health you know."

Gin told Scrooge to take a look around the bar, inspect the faces, the smiles, the low-cut tops and the frilly skirts. Scrooge did this. He also took note of what was struggling to remain inside said tops and skirts.

He spotted his younger self standing against a wall. Obviously the wall needed him to hold it up, as every girl who approached him to dance was sent away. Scrooge wished he had asked someone else to hold the wall instead.

As the fiddler continued to play, his energy levels kept in check by the Red Bull intravenous drip attached to his arm, the room appeared to come alive. This was confirmed when it blew a shower of snot from its nose on the ceiling.

Scrooge watched as Fezziwig made merry with his wife. They should really have waited until they were alone. Fezziwig passed alcohol around like it was water and someone used it to wash their feet which were covered in snot from the ceiling. Scrooge noted Fezziwig's generosity. This was a man who would, on a working day, drive his employees into the ground then make them pay for a spade to dig themselves out.

Fezziwig's guests danced and danced to the joyful music. By now the fiddler had been joined by a small travelling band of accordionists. According to the accordionists the fiddler was still fiddling with more than just his fiddle and later that evening he was found with his bow inside a maid's music box.

As the night progressed, the bar almost ran dry and the partygoers were pissed as newts. The dancing became more frantic, in some cases obscene, and many had danced their feet off.

Fezziwig had retired to a chair by the front door. He would much rather have retired to the south of France. As his guests began to leave, Fezziwig made sure they all collected their feet on the way out and wished them all a joyful Christmas

Anthony Lund

before pleasantly pushing them out into the freezing night with a big smile on his face.

"Spirit?" Scrooge said, turning to look for his spectral companion. "Spirit?"

Scrooge searched the room, finally focusing on the ghost who was lying on the bar attempting to grab hold of the ale pump without much success. Scrooge crossed the room then he ticked it and put a circle around it for good measure. Drunken revellers passed through him with every step he took...it was still something he was getting used to.

"Spirit, I want to leave here," Scrooge said to the frustrated ghost.

"I want a bloody drink but sometimes we don't always get what we want!" Gin said sourly. "What's up? Conscience getting to you? I saw Jiminy Cricket hopping by before but I thought he was looking for that long nosed freak he normally hangs around with."

"No my conscience is fine," Scrooge said.

"Why? Did you give it to someone else?"

"Just take me away from here."

Gin sat up. "You're not feeling a bit guilty about something are you?"

Scrooge squirmed. "No. Why should I?"

"I'm sure your nose is bigger than it was before. Are you certain that Cricket wasn't looking for you?"

"I have nothing to be ashamed of!"

"Your bottom lip is trembling again," Gin said, putting a Polo mint in his mouth. "Is it because of how happy Fezziwig made people? How for so little expense he could treat his employees and neighbours to a good Christmas knees up?"

"How can you say that was little expense?" Scrooge exclaimed. "They sucked Dick's bar dry! He's sitting over there now with a lopsided grin on his face. It's exhaustion clearly! All that had to be paid for in some way."

"Well," Gin said, rubbing his temple. "Actually Fezziwig was arrested for theft not long after you left the company. It seems he had been frequently intercepting The Black Bull's brewery deliveries in order to run his parties. He was done on three counts of possession, and one count of performing a sex act at a public function."

"The thieving bastard," Scrooge said. "What a penny-pinching, tight-fisted little…"

Scrooge closed his mouth. An awkward silence lingered. It looked twelve years old and was trying to hide a porn magazine behind its back.

"You were saying?" Gin asked casually.

"Nothing."

"So you weren't thinking you should have perhaps treated your little clerk to a small Christmas drink?"

"No I bloody well wasn't! Do I look like a charity?"

"In your state they'd have closed you down. Anyway, my time here is growing short."

Anthony Lund

"You look the same size to me," Scrooge commented.

"You really think you're a funny fucker, don't you?"

Gin clicked his fingers and the bar melted away.

Scrooge found himself standing in a puddle and the ground around him was covered in snow. He vaguely recognised the area from his younger days. He also recognised his younger self from his younger days, which were now the olden days. It was very confusing wandering around in his own past.

"When you have finished with your sarcastic remarks, Mr Chuckles, this is almost the last stop," the Spirit said, picking his nose in search of something interesting. "Take note, it's a real heartbreaker this one."

"I already know the ending. I don't want to watch"

"You went to see Titanic didn't you? Stop moaning and pay attention."

Scrooge looked across to where his younger self sat on a park bench. Beside him was a young girl, very pretty and with big boobs. Scrooge felt something move in his heart.

"Will you stop doing that!" Scrooge said to the ghost.

"It's so addictive though. At least I can say you seem to be in working order in there anyway. I do feel that the heart may have been broken though."

"Are you meant to be this cruel?"

"Well I do have to make my visit memorable."

On the park bench, the girl was sobbing. Tears were rolling down her cheeks and dripping off her chin. A lake was gathering in the tightly squeezed swell of her mighty cleavage, and a midget was fishing in it.

Young Scrooge was watching her. He was watching her tits more closely.

"I'm sorry it had to end like this," he said to them.

"Are you sure there is no way to continue?" the girl said through the sobbing.

"I don't see how it can. They have announced there will definitely be no more episodes of The Office."

"I can't believe it. Such terrible news, and on the day I chose to tell you you're dumped as well."

"Yes, a bit of a pisser all round really. Although you still have not told me why you want to end it."

"I didn't end it," the girl said. "It was the producers of the show who decided not to make any more."

"I meant our relationship," Scrooge said with patience.

"Oh, that. You've changed Scrooge. Your love of money has clouded your actions and turned you into another. You're not the man you were when I met you."

"Who am I then?"

"Ebenezer Scrooge of course."

"So who was I when we met?"

"A different Ebenezer Scrooge."

Young Scrooge scratched his head. "I'm so pleased we cleared that up."

Anthony Lund

In the lake of the girl's breasts, the midget yelled with delight as he got a bite.

"I am too," the girl said. "But it does not change anything I have said. Our relationship must end as I know you are unable to give up your ruthless business streak."

"And that is the only reason?" Scrooge asked. "You are ending it just because of that?"

"Well now you come to mention it, you pick your nose, you fart in bed and waft the covers in my face chanting "Get a snort of that!", you lick the whole chocolate bar before offering me any, and then there's your enormous cock waking me up every morning!"

"I can't help that. It's just doing what all cocks do. You know it was a present from Farmer Tomlin and it would be rude to give it back."

"You always manage to have an answer, Scrooge."

"You always ask such simple questions."

The girl wiped away her tears and loosened her corset to drain the lake. The midget was drowned as his boat capsized and he was washed away on the tide. She stood up.

"Goodbye, Scrooge. I hope one day you will find happiness."

"I hope one day I find a genie in a lamp. Goodbye."

The girl walked away, her feet squelching with lake water. Young Scrooge watched from the bench. Old Scrooge watched from the pathway. Between them they saw her breasts from all angles.

"Well, that was a maudlin moment wasn't it?" Gin said.

"You're a little shit."

"I have trophies to prove it. That was the only person you ever loved. And she broke your heart into an impossible jigsaw puzzle. She may as well have ripped it out of your chest and hacked it up with—"

"Ok, ok. I get the message."

"She was really happy after she left you, you know. Married some really rich stuck-up ponce with a big wallet, big house, and he was endowed with her type of enormous co—"

"Enough!" Scrooge said. "I don't want to know."

"I bet she knew. It must have been like a baseball bat going in."

"You are a demon, torturing me with my past. Take me home. Leave me be."

"In that order?"

"Yes in that order. I want to be rid of you."

"Almost, Scrooge," Gin said. "One more sight to see."

The Ghost poked Scrooge in both eyes with candy cigarettes. When Scrooge could see again, the park had been left behind and they were once more indoors.

The room bounced with activity. Children screamed and laughed and played and danced. Annoying little bastards to their mother who was trying to read in a chair by the fire. She would

Anthony Lund

remember to take the pill in future. Sitting beside her was a girl Scrooge almost recognised. It was she of the big boobs...but no, that was not quite true. Scrooge realised his big boobed beauty was actually the mother of the girl, aged and seemingly living a thriving family life.

There came a knocking at the door, and the children's father burst into the room with gifts up to his eyebrows. He walked into the room and tripped over the baby as it crawled by.

Without waiting a blink, the thousand and one children pounced upon their stricken father, tearing at gift wrap and clothes alike.

Childish screams and shouts mixed with grunts and curses as the father of the horde attempted to escape the tempest of hands and mouths. An excited voice yelled "I got a snake!" before his father pulled it out of the child's hand and tucked it back in his trousers.

"Belle, my dearest, darling hunny-bun," the husband said to he wife when he was finally free. "I saw a friend of yours today. Guess who it was!"

His wife, she of the original big boobs sitting opposite her eldest offspring who clearly took after her mother, said, "Dangling Dan?"

"No."

"Big Willie?"

"No."

"Hung Harry?"

"Erm...no. Have I met any of these people?"

"No dear, I think you were out when they were here."

Her husband ran a hand though his blond hair then ruffled the blonde hair of his wife.

Three of his children ran up and clung to his leg. He ruffled their little auburn, brown and black heads and told them to run along.

"Actually it was Mr Scrooge," he said, watching his many-coloured haired children playing around him. "He was sitting in his office when I walked past. Working on a Christmas Eve! Did you know that partner of his is expected to die tonight? I'm sure there is no one else as alone as that bugger."

"Oh, of course I remember Scrooge," Belle said. "I would have probably married him had things been different. I never even got my hands on his enormous wad."

Her husband was counting the number of children who shared his hair colour and was still on his first finger.

"Tell me," he said to this wife. "When did we last have sex?"

"That would be on our wedding night, dear. That was the only time."

"Oh," her husband responded over the hollering of their many offspring. "That's what I thought."

"Spirit!" Scrooge said. "I want this to be done with! I can't take any more."

Gin picked bits of toffee from his teeth.

Anthony Lund

"It's no good blaming me. All of this is from your past. It's already happened. You can't do anything about it."

"I can try to forget about it if some sweet-toothed little bastard stops reminding me about it!"

The Spirit sat up and looked at its wrist. "Hmm. Well it is time to go actually. I've got you on a strict curfew."

"Hey that's my watch!" Scrooge shouted as the park faded around them.

Scrooge leaped onto the Spirit, one hand grasping at his stolen watch while the other reached for the ghost's throat.

"What are you going to do?" Gin asked. "Kill me?"

Scrooge watched as Gin's face altered, taking on the faces of his own past and mocking him with them. Above the Spirit's head its light burned brighter than ever.

"You're going to blind me in a minute!" Scrooge snapped. "Give me that."

He pulled the large candle extinguisher from Gin's hand, and brought it down squarely on the ghost's head.

"Let's see how you like this!" Scrooge bellowed in triumph as he forced the extinguisher further and further down.

The ghost shrieked like a girl. "Help! I'm shrinking, shrinking! What a world, what a world!"

Down, down still deeper down Scrooge pressed. Louder and louder the ghost screamed. Darker and darker the room became. Sillier and sillier the sentences were written.

A Christmas Carol - Retold

"Bah! Strawberry creams!" Scrooge shouted in a final moment of triumph.

The last of the light vanished beneath the extinguisher, the ghost's voice faded and Scrooge suddenly realised he was back in his own room.

The realisation brought with it a tiredness Scrooge had never experienced before. Within moments he was face down on his bed in a pool of his own drool, muttering about big breasts, large wads and huge melons.

Stave III

Vodka - The Presently
Hungry Spirit

Scrooge sat up and pushed back his covers.

The curtains around his bed were closed and he had no way of knowing what time it was. Somehow though, the first hour of a new morning seemed the most likely option.

This time he did not doubt that he could have slept all day. There was something about fighting a watch-thieving Spirit that made the senses acute to such things. If he was right, the second of Marley's Spirits would be soon peeping through the curtains and assaulting him with confectionary.

"Not this time," Scrooge muttered.

He reached for the nearest curtain and wildly pulled it open.

"Boo!" he yelled at the empty room.

Undeterred he moved across to the foot of his bed and once again whipped open the curtain.

"Aha!"

A Christmas Carol – Retold

Still nothing. Scrooge shuffled to the other side of the bed, stood up in all his naked glory and tore the curtain down from its rail.

"Gotcha!"

A shocked burglar stood on tiptoes, his hand outstretched to an ornament on Scrooge's bedside table. The next moment he crashed through the window in a panic, the echo of the word "Pervert" following in his wake.

"Well now I'm really pissed off," Scrooge said, sitting back down his bed and pulling on a nightshirt.

Scrooge remained still, waiting patiently for the appearance of the next Spirit. He propped himself up against his headboard, making sure that whatever came to him would not catch him unawares.

He prepared himself for anything from the Stay Puft Marshmallow Man to a tap dancing turd. Even in the case of the latter, Scrooge was determined that this time he wouldn't be taking any shit from the manifestation.

The chime of one echoed in Scrooge's ear loud enough to deafen him. He moved the clock away from his face and replaced it on the bedside table. He had picked it up to ensure he did not miss the hour and in that, at least, his plan had succeeded.

Then the one occurrence Scrooge had not anticipated happened.

Nothing.

Anthony Lund

No apparition made itself known and for fifteen minutes Scrooge sat biting his nails.

When he was down to the second knuckle a sudden realisation came to him. The room was lighter than it should have been.

"If it's that bastard burglar again I'll —"

Scrooge was not allowed to voice what he would do to the spherical extremities of any thief's person as the door before him opened up and a brilliant light spilled out. It washed over the floor and this time it did stain his rug.

"That better not be on my bloody electricity bill," Scrooge shouted into the light. "And why the hell can I smell turkey?"

Scrooge moved into the light, squinting to see what was in his sitting room and how much of a mess it had made on his chairs. If Marley dared ask him for any money then he would send an invoice of his own for his watch and whatever else went missing over the night.

Blindly feeling his way through the room, Scrooge caught his foot in a bit of carpet, staggered forward and felt the solid edge of a table connect with his groin. He groaned and slid to the floor where he landed on a plate of jelly.

"Steady there, Old Man," a voice in the light boomed. Somewhere a window shattered under the pressure.

Scrooge rubbed a hand against his injury. "Will you do something about that goddamned light? And less of the old man stuff!'

71

The light went out.

"Funny. I can't see any more now than I could when – bugger it!"

A low light illuminated the room. Scrooge was holding his head.

"That table is a hazard," he said. "I expect you're going to take it with you when you go?"

Scrooge was finally able to view his latest arrival for the first time. He thought he would wait for the second time to look at him properly as he was too big to view in one sitting.

"Good evening, Scrooge," the large figure boomed. "I am Vodka, the Ghost of Christmas Present. I am always stuck in the here and now."

"Where's the here and now?"

"Six miles south of the where and when."

Scrooge had a thought. "They don't keep any spare thumbs there do they?"

"Not that I know of," Vodka replied. "I would simply say you should have been more careful with the ones you had."

Scrooge looked hard at the ghost. He always found it hard looking at ghosts. Vodka was about nine feet tall and as broad as an obese elephant. His feet were bare, hairy and in need of a wash and he carried a large torch that seemed to burn but somehow did not set off the smoke alarm. He sported a big red beard, big red mop of hair, was wearing a big red coat and held a big red book.

Anthony Lund

"Ebenezer Scrooge. This is your Christmas Life."

"Fabulous," Scrooge said. "Just what I was hoping for. Whatever will it say about my wonderful way of living?"

"I'll hit you with it if you don't shut up."

Scrooge decided to close his mouth for a while. He had often heard that vodka gave you a headache and now he knew why.

"I expect you have never seen anything like me before," Vodka said, just as an unexpected breeze blew open his robe, revealing what Scrooge first thought was a family sized Bratwurst.

"You are right," Scrooge said. "I have never seen anything like it in my life."

"And you have not walked with any of my brothers?"

"Not that I know of. Are there many of them?"

"Oh no," the Spirit said. "Only eighteen hundred."

"Fuck me!" Scrooge said.

"You know that was my mother's favourite phrase," Vodka said. "I think father took her a little too literally at times. Now, are you ready for a little journey?" the Spirit asked.

Scrooge responded with a nod.

"Very well then. We'll begin."

"Hang on a minute," Scrooge said against his better judgement. "What's the point of all this?"

Scrooge gestured the room around him which had been transformed into a Harrod's Christmas Grotto.

A Christmas Carol – Retold

It was still his living room, but it looked like Alan Titchmarsh had given it a makeover. The walls were hung with ivy and holly, red berries glistening in the midst of so much green. In the fire place a blaze was stocked with more coal and logs than Scrooge would have used in a dozen millennia. Around the floor were scattered large boxes wrapped in outlandish paper and topped with magnificent bows.

Then there was the table that had given him more injuries than any other inanimate object he had encountered. Its surface was covered in a variety of delicious looking dishes. Each delicious dish contained equally delicious looking food including the turkey that had spread its smell throughout the house quicker than a skunk on a moped, apple pies, custard, roast potatoes, sausages, Christmas pudding, crumbles and pastries. Scrooge did not need reminding that there was more food on the floor – the sticky mess on his trousers was testament to that.

"Oh that's just for decoration," Vodka said. "Although I have to say I do occasionally have a little nibble at a few things."

"Really? How do you stay so slim?"

The sound of the big red book connecting with Scrooge's head was like someone playing a single beat on a base drum.

"I'm sure there are laws against doing that!" Scrooge said.

"I'll do it again if you don't pipe down."

"I'll be good."

Anthony Lund

"You'd better believe you will. Now take hold of my robe."

Scrooge did so and the Spirit clapped his chunky hands together. The foundations of the house trembled and Scrooge felt his internal organs bouncing off his ribs like pinballs. He closed his eyes to blink and when they opened again he was no longer in his home.

Scrooge found himself standing in the middle of a street that was covered in snow. Beside him Vodka bit into a turkey leg.

"What kind of host are you?" Scrooge asked, glaring at the Spirit so hard the turkey began to sizzle.

"What?!" the Spirit replied.

"First you turn my bedroom into a banquet hall, then you bring me out into the street without a coat and then you stand there stuffing your face while my stomach thinks of turning cannibal and eating my liver!"

The Spirit removed the turkey leg from his mouth with a loud slurp. "Sorry. Want some?"

Scrooge looked at the offered leg. He watched a long string of drool dangle off the end of it.

"I think I'll pass," Scrooge said. "Why are we here anyway? It's a bit of a hole."

"No, it's a full hole. We're both standing in it."

"So we are. Why are we standing in a hole?"

"It was here when we arrived."

"Is there any point to this conversation?"

"Not really, but it has been fun."

Scrooge looked about him. The town was not exactly a cheerful place. The houses were dreary and bleak, very few decorations hung from windows and a heavy mist filled the air. Even to Scrooge it was bloody depressing.

Yet somehow, the people around them were still cheerful. They sang as they scraped snow from their roofs and paths, as they removed ice from their windows and as they removed their frozen pets from deep piles of snow. Along the road, shops were open, their owners standing outside to usher people inside where they could be made to part with what little money they had – something that Scrooge appreciated more than anything else he had seen so far – and bantered with each other across the dirty road. In the shop windows goods were on display for all to drool at as they walked by until someone slipped on a particularly thick patch of saliva and the owner was forced to pull down the blinds for safety purposes.

As Scrooge and the Spirit stood, the bells of a church began to chime and like extras from a living dead movie the people emerged from doorways, alleyways, pubs, shops, sewer grates and brothels to make their way towards the source of the noise. All had annoyingly gleeful expressions on their face, which were inexplicable to Scrooge with the exception of those leaving the brothels.

Scrooge was aware that the Spirit was taking a great interest of these people as they passed by. Frequently, as people passed holding food the Spirit would lift the lids of the dishes, have a quick taste of what was underneath then sprinkle something powdery from his torch over the rest.

"I thought I had no morals!" Scrooge muttered.

For a moment Scrooge considered the Spirit's torch. It was certainly no ordinary torch, but then again nothing of recent events could be described as ordinary. If the torch had turned out to be battery operated it would have been something of a disappointment. Occasionally people would pass by speaking heatedly, and with just a quick sprinkle from the torch their quarrels were forgotten.

Scrooge could not prevent himself thinking how much money could be made from such an item. It seemed you could bottle happiness…although he doubted the Spirit would appreciate the business opportunity in quite the same way. He seemed more of a duty free Spirit.

"Does that stuff you sprinkle from your torch have a particular flavour?" Scrooge asked.

"It does. When people eat it will be like they are swallowing a little mouthful of me."

"That just sounds perverse. You spread yourself around a bit don't you?"

"Everyone should be able to have me for Christmas. And those who cannot afford luxury receive just a little more than the others."

"Why? If they cannot afford luxury then why are you giving them one?"

"Now who sounds perverse?"

"Eh?" Scrooge asked, replaying his last sentence in his head. "I didn't mean it like that!"

"Of course you didn't. To answer your question though, the poor need it more than anyone else. Now, let us walk a little."

They walked a little. It didn't take long.

"Now," Vodka said. "Don't you know that house?"

"Which one?"

"The one you don't know."

"If I don't know which one then how can I say whether I know it or not?"

"Do you know any of the houses?"

"No."

"Then it doesn't matter which one I mean does it?"

Scrooge felt another headache coming on and Vodka wasn't helping.

"Which house are we going to?" Scrooge sighed.

"E mnn em anm unim."

Scrooge looked around to find the Spirit eating another turkey leg.

"Did your mother never tell you not to speak with your mouth full?"

Anthony Lund

The Spirit swallowed then dropped to his knees as the turkey bone lodged itself in his throat. His chubby hands pounded his chest and his face turned an unhealthy shade of blue.

Scrooge watched the performance without emotion. "I didn't know ghosts could choke."

Vodka stopped gagging and his face turned from blue to red in an instant. "Sorry, I sometimes forget."

"So which house again?"

"Don't you know that—"

"We've already done that bit," Scrooge said, folding his arms neatly and putting them to one side to be ironed.

"Oh. Right. Well it's this one."

Scrooge surveyed the building before him without much interest. It was not the kind of place he would call a house. It was more a very elaborate cardboard box with a door and windows. Hanging on the door was a holly wreath similar to the one Scrooge had last seen decorating his nephew like a neck brace. There was also a knocker. The collectors obviously hadn't called yet.

"So why's this one important? Who lives here?"

"Santa Clause," said the Spirit.

"What?"

"It's Bob Cratchit's house, you old fool. Only someone who works for you would have to live in a place like this."

"I work for me and I don't live in a place like this," Scrooge said defiantly.

"I think you have a slight unfair advantage in that respect."

"Fair point. Are we actually going inside or just standing on the doorstep all night?"

"I sense you are feeling keen to go inside and learn a lesson from your employee," the Spirit said.

"I sense I'm losing feeling in my toes and want to get inside where it's warmer."

"Hmm, there must be something wrong with my teleporter. You shouldn't be able to feel the cold."

"You shouldn't be able to stuff your face with turkey but you managed it."

"Touché."

Scrooge and the Spirit entered the Cratchit house through the wall and found themselves standing in the fireplace. The fire was burning merrily.

"This is quite uncomfortable," Scrooge said. "My feet are cooking."

"Nothing stopping you moving is there?"

"Yes."

"What?"

"My burning feet. Have you tried walking on hot coals?"

The Spirit thought for a moment while Scrooge continued to singe. "Well you're already standing on them so I don't suppose walking on them will be much different."

"I hadn't thought about it like that," Scrooge conceded.

Anthony Lund

"Obviously," the Spirit said, toasting a forkful of marshmallows.

Scrooge stepped out of the fireplace and stamped out the flames creeping up his leg.

Mrs Cratchit and two of the children, Belinda and Peter, were gathered around a small dining table in the middle of the floor. The table appeared to be laid out for a light snack, but Scrooge had a feeling this was not the case. People did not usually gather around a table wearing paper hats unless they were celebrating something or were in an asylum.

"Doesn't look much does it?" The Ghost of Christmas Present said, popping a hot marshmallow in his mouth.

"I thought I was meant to be the ruthless swine here?"

"What do you mean?"

"There's not enough food on that table to feed one let alone a whole family and you're chomping on marshmallows!"

The Ghost looked slightly embarrassed but continued to chew. "They can't see me."

"Minor detail," Scrooge said. "I can see you and I'm bloody starving!"

"You should have said earlier," Vodka said, tossing another fluffy lump into his mouth. "That was the last one."

"If you weren't dead, I'd kill you."

"If I weren't dead we wouldn't be here!"

Scrooge rubbed his temple. "Ok, let's stop now. You have too many paradoxes for my liking."

The pair returned to watching the Cratchit family like a peculiar pair of badger watchers.

"Your father will be back soon," Mrs Cratchit said to the gathered children.

"Thank god," said her son Peter. "The dinner is cold! He does it every year. Takes Tim to church then instead of coming straight back he always has to go singing and dancing around the streets."

"Peter, we know your dad is a nutcase but he's the only one you have so shut up and make do."

The front door opened and the family turned expectedly, only to find Martha standing there.

"Oh," they said as one.

"Well that's a fine welcome," Martha said. "I'll just go home if you feel like that."

"No, dear," Mrs Cratchit said. "We're just waiting for you father. He's late again."

"He's late every year. He always goes dancing–"

"Yes, Martha, we know," Mrs Cratchit cut in. "Why don't you hide in the cupboard and surprise him when he gets here."

"Bollocks to that, mother. I'm not sitting in there until he shows up. How old do you think I am? Five?"

"Fair point I suppose. Anyway, you've put on weight. I'm not sure your fat arse would fit in there any more."

"Mother!" Martha gasped. "I'm not fat! I'll show you."

Anthony Lund

Martha stormed over to the cupboard, pulled open the door and climbed inside. She closed the door with a bang, which made a change to using the handle.

"See, I can fit in no problem," the cupboard said in Martha's muffled voice.

"So you can, dear," Mrs Cratchit said. "Now just stay in there a couple of minutes, I can hear your father coming."

"You sneaky bitch," the cupboard said.

The front door opened again and Bob came staggering through under the weight of his extra long scarf and Tiny Tim, who rode his shoulders like a champion jockey.

"Ok, son," Bob said. "You don't have to use your crutch as a whip anymore."

"Sorry, dad," Tim said standing on his fathers shoulders, putting a fist in the air and diving off. He landed with a crunch on the stone floor.

"You let him watch Superman last night, didn't you?" Mrs Cratchit said, shaking her head. "How many times have I told you not to let him watch anything like that? His medication makes him think he can do silly things."

"Sorry, I forgot."

"And you know when he bounces off the floor like that it sets his Tourettes off something rotten."

"I know, dear."

Bob scooped Tim off the stone floor and dropped him into the empty chair at the table.

"Thanks, Dad. You wan– " Tiny Tim said as a large Brussels sprout was slapped into his mouth.

"It's no problem, son. Now, where is our Martha?"

"She said she cannot come today," Mrs Cratchit said.

"What? Not coming?" Bob said in aghast horror as though he had not gone through the same farce every year.

The cupboard door swung open and Martha ran out.

"I'm here, father!" she yelled in fake euphoria before jumping on her dad.

Bob tried to hold his feet but it was no good. He was a small man and his daughter was tall and well proportioned.

"I think we may have to give this a miss next year," Bob said from under her proportions.

Martha lifted herself off her father then helped him to his feet.

Bob took his seat at the table and picked up the knife waiting for him. He looked at the turkey for a moment, as if contemplating whether to cut it or just eat it in one mouthful. Scrooge had seen bigger canaries.

"Well," said Bob to the table. "Here's another glorious Christmas day."

Mrs Cratchit looked at her husband. "Bob, how many times do I have to tell you the table isn't listening to you?"

"Sorry, dear."

"Mum," said Belinda. "Is dad going potty?"

"No, hunny, his trousers always have that dark patch."

Anthony Lund

"Actually these are the ones without the patch," Bob said.

There was a moment of silence while the family digested the implications of this.

"I think I'll finish dishing out dinner, darling," Mrs Cratchit said, taking the knife from her husband and wiping it on her apron.

Bob sat down and picked up a glass of wine so cheap it was actually vinegar. "Well while you're serving up I'd like to make a toast."

"You nearly set the house on fire last time," his wife said. "Besides we've already used the bread that hadn't gone green."

"In that case, I'll raise my glass instead. To Mr Scrooge, the man who made this feast possible."

"Yes, he made it possibly the smallest feast in history. In fact, you could be done under Trade Descriptions for calling it that so be careful."

"If it wasn't for Mr Scrooge though, we wouldn't even have this."

"You're right. If you worked for anyone else we'd probably have that great monster goose you dribble over all the time in the poulterer's window."

Bob's tongue lolled as his mind turned to the giant bird. "Mmm...goose."

A Christmas Carol – Retold

"Snap out of it," Mrs Cratchit said. "It's not going to happen so stop getting hot and bothered over it. How was Tim in church today?"

"He was good as gold. Well apart from when the vicar was naming the Holy Trinity and Tim said the father, the son and the holy shit."

The Cratchit children giggled, earning a disapproving look from their father.

Mrs Cratchit finished cutting the turkey, and dividing up the vegetable equally. Once they were equal she gave everyone a different amount. She sat down opposite her husband and they ate their meal in silence.

Less than a minute later they began the washing up.

"Who wants pudding?" Bob asked the children.

"All of us," Martha said. "Unless we want to starve."

"I only have two hands!" Mrs Cratchit said. "I'll get it out of the oven in a minute."

Around the table the Cratchits waited like birds in a nest; mouths open, tongues out.

Soon Mrs Cratchit appeared holding a round pot containing a steaming Christmas pudding the size of a baseball.

The faces around the table continued to grin despite the secret thoughts of eating each other that lurked in their minds. Maybe the grins were of insanity rather than happiness.

"What a beautiful pudding!" Bob exclaimed. "The best since we've been married."

Anthony Lund

"That's because I got it from Tesco," Mrs Cratchit said. "You know mine come out like lumps of coal."

"You mean you knew they were bad all this time and yet you kept making them every year?"

"Well no one complained about them did they?"

The family declined to comment. So much indigestion had passed over the years that they did not want to remember.

"Well let us enjoy this one while we have it," Bob said. "Remember, children, one spoonful each until we make sure everyone has some."

Bob reached over for his glass and raised it in the air again.

"Bob," she said. "If you mention Scrooge again as the founder of the feast, we'll be feasting on you in a few hours."

Bob started to lower his glass then a light bulb came on in the dark attic of his head. Someone had just rented out the space where his brain used to be.

"Merry Christmas to all," he said. "And God bless us."

The children all looked to their mother for approval. She nodded and they all echoed the toast.

Tiny Tim raised his glass last. To his left, Mrs Cratchit picked up a spare sprout.

"God bless us every one. Fuc— "

The sprout hit its mark.

"Poor child," Scrooge said. "Such a terrible affliction."

"Everyone swears these days," Vodka remarked, taking a swig from a bottle of champagne. "You can't walk down the street these days without someone giving you a fuck."

"I think you need to be more careful about which streets you walk down. Try to avoid the ones with red lights."

"I didn't say I was complaining."

"I think you need some kind of counselling."

"Are we ready to move on?" Vodka asked.

"Tell me first, is Tim ok? He looks a little off colour."

"Scrooge," the Spirit said in a friendly, slightly patronising tone. "You've seen how much food he has eaten. You've watched him throw himself off his father's shoulders in a moment of hallucination. You can see that he is not in the greatest physical condition. Now let me ask you...do you think he is ok?"

"He could be worse, I guess."

"Well how about if I told you that I see there will soon be an empty chair at the table."

"Oh," Scrooge said. "That's great news! It will mean there will be more food to go around and Tim will surely perk up a bit."

"It is his chair that will be empty, Scrooge."

"Is he going on a school trip?"

The Spirit pulled a face of despair then pushed it back into shape.

Anthony Lund

"Scrooge, the boy will die unless something drastic changes in the future."

"Are you sure?"

"You know, I'd heard that you were really dense but I didn't have any idea it was so true. If nothing happens to change the future then I am certain he will die, as certain as I know that soon I will not be able to resist the temptation to smack you over the head with the book again."

"Wow, you're really sure, aren't you?"

"Yes."

Scrooge lowered his head. When it touched the floor he pulled it back up.

"Now," Vodka said. "It is time to go."

"Can't we stay and watch them just a little longer?"

Around the table the family began to sing a very out of tune version of Jingle Bells.

"Never mind!" Scrooge yelled pulling the Spirit's robes like a bell rope. "Go-go-go-let's-go!"

"I thought you might see it that way," Vodka said. "By the way, how do you manage to hold on to things so well without any thumbs?"

The Spirit clapped his hands before waiting for a reply. Scrooge felt his ears pop.

They were once again outside, though the sky was darker and more snow had fallen. In the houses around them lights burned and fires blazed against the cool of the approaching night.

"Never mind the cool of the approaching night. It's bloody freezing!"

In the houses around them lights burned and fires blazed against the bloody freezing cold outside.

"A much better description."

"Who are you talking to?" Vodka asked.

"You wouldn't understand," Scrooge said. "If I told you that all Spirits are nothing but figments of imagination in books and movies what would you say?"

"Huh?"

"Exactly, so it's probably best you don't ask questions and just stick to the story."

"I won't even pretend to know what you're talking about and I'll put it down to your overworked mind."

"Good," Scrooge said.

They continued along the road, passing the joyful sounds drifting from taverns and the skipping lamp lighters who were living up to their name. They passed Bob the Butcher, Tommy the Tailor and Roger the Barman, who incidentally was also living up to his name.

Suddenly the street vanished beneath them and was replaced with dirt and stones. Scrooge looked up against the biting wind to find they stood on a deserted moor. The sky was

Anthony Lund

almost black and the cold was holding Scrooge in an icy embrace.

"Will you get off me!" he said, slapping the cold away like a bad dog. To the Spirit he said, "Now where are we?"

"This is a small place where Miners live. Yet despite working in the darkness of the underground tunnels, they still know me."

"You? Have you visited them as well?"

"No, you nerk. I mean they know the present, they know what is happening now. They know it is Christmas time."

"Oh."

A short distance away a light shone from a hut and the Spirit led them towards it. Inside an old man and his family sat around a small fire and joyously sang carols despite the desolate howling wind outside.

The Spirit did not wait here, but told Scrooge to take hold of his robe again. Soon they were zooming over the land at a hundred miles an hour until they were pulled for speeding and given a £60 fine.

To avoid any further fines, the ghost took Scrooge out to sea in a beautiful boat the colour of runny snot. They travelled across the black sea passing lighthouses and small boats adrift on the choppy waves where Christmas had not failed to touch their lives.

Scrooge closed his eyes for a moment, wondering at how people so isolated could be so happy without the use of drugs or alcohol or a big breasted beauty called Brenda who liked to take charge, when he heard a sudden burst of laughter he recognised.

"Nephew?" Scrooge said, opening his eyes to find they were no longer flying.

They were once again indoors, but now a long way it seemed from the Cratchit house. This house was far better decorated, warmer and didn't have the slight smell of urine that had underlined the air in the Cratchits'.

"Why have you brought me here?" Scrooge asked. "Of all places! Why here?"

"Because we're not doing this for fun, remember?"

Scrooge found himself staring at the bright-cheeked, holly wreath-scarred face of his nephew. He guessed they were in the sitting room as no one was standing despite there being a lot of people present. Some of them Scrooge vaguely recognised, which as they were his relatives he thought he really aught to.

His nephew was laughing like a loon, and it seemed whenever he laughed so did most of the room. It was like an infection. Scrooge did not feel like laughing. Miserable sod.

"The old fart wouldn't even take my holly wreath!" Scrooge's nephew told the crowd.

"Well bully for him," Scrooge's niece chirped in.

She was very much a beauty was Scrooge's niece. Her face was bright and shining with an amazing light. She had a cute little nose, lovely lips and big round eyes that were full of youthful wonder. Then of course there were her...

Anthony Lund

"Knockers!" Scrooge's nephew continued. "I don't lie. They stole his knockers from his very doors! You know I don't care how much of a goat he is, there is nothing worse than having your knockers pinched."

"Oh I don't know," Scrooge's nephew's brother-in-law's drunken friend piped up. "I've had my bell pulled off before."

"Humphrey," Scrooge's nephew said. "You paid her for that."

"Oh, yes, well, erm…anyway what were we talking about?"

"My Uncle Scrooge. I believe that he is a silly fool for declining my offer to eat and be merry with us. Never fear though, I will continue to go to him year after year until he sees his error and decides to come and eat with us. Even if he should die before it happens I will not allow a Christmas to go by unless I at least try to make him see sense. Maybe if nothing else then he might see fit to pay that clerk of his a decent bonus!"

"How much have you had to drink?" Scrooge's niece asked him. "You know it won't happen, any of it. Now let's forget about Ebenezer Scrooge for a while and eat."

"I bet you feel really wanted at this moment," Vodka said.

Scrooge did not reply.

After their meal, they played some music, sang some songs and a couple snuck away to make their own music and tickle the ivories in a different way. Games were played in both areas. In the sitting room, a game of blind man's buff ensued, which as always was nothing more than a good excuse for drunken men to grope someone other than their partner and suffer no consequences.

When all had been squeezed, nipped, tickled and poked, they changed the game. Scrooge moved around the room to get a better look at what exactly they were doing. All attention seemed to have moved to his nephew who was crouched down in front of the fire pretending to be something that, to Scrooge, seemed to be a constipated frog.

"Is it a constipated frog?" someone shouted from a chair.

"You're right!" said Scrooge's nephew standing up.

"What are they doing?" Scrooge asked the Spirit.

"Charades," Vodka replied, plunging his spoon into a toffee pudding.

"Where did you...never mind. I hope you choke on it."

"I can't choke, remember?"

"Funny fucker," Scrooge mumbled.

The jovial atmosphere continued with a game of How, When and Where. Scrooge's niece was a natural, spilling out clues and questions then guessing speedily the clues posed by others. Scrooge also shouted out answers against his better judgement. He didn't want to enjoy himself, but somehow he could not help but become involved in the game. The Spirit watched in mild amusement as Scrooge became engrossed in the proceedings and every now and then leaned across to wipe the drool from Scrooge's chin.

Anthony Lund

After a time Scrooge's nephew clapped his hands. "Ok let's play a different game. We'll play the Yes/No game."

"I didn't know Des O'Conner was here." someone said. "I'd have brought ear plugs."

"Not that Yes/No game," Scrooge's nephew said. "We don't have a gong. You ask me questions about whom or what I am, and I can only answer yes or no. Then you have to guess."

"Why not call it the 'Ask me questions about whom or what I am and I'll answer yes or no until you guess' game," said a small Irish voice in the corner of the room.

"Who let O'Donnell loose on the Guinness?"

"Hey, I'm not drunk. 'Tis just me Irish wit."

"It's something that rhymes with wit but that's as far as it goes. Now to the game. Someone ask me a question."

"What colour underwear do you have on?"

"A relevant question," Scrooge's nephew said. "And one I can answer yes or no to."

"Can you only say yes?" O'Donnell slurred.

"No."

"Can you say no as well?"

"Yes."

"Yer der yes/no man, so you are!"

"O'Donnell I'm going to give you a dry slap in a minute."

"'Tis just my Irish–"

A Christmas Carol – Retold

The little Irishman didn't see the Guinness bottle until it smacked him in the face. His father had always told him the drink would get him in the end.

"Ok, a sensible question now."

"Are you a man?" Scrooge's niece asked.

"Yes."

"Are you miserable?"

"Yes."

"Are you the inspiration for Victor Meldrew?"

"Yes. Have you been going to telepathy class again?"

"Are you a tight-fisted, penny-pinching old bollock who calls himself an uncle then assaults you with a holly wreath before kicking you out of his Counting House into the street, where you fell flat on your face before being run over by a horse and carriage?"

Scrooge's nephew winced and felt the hoof print on his back. "Yes."

Silence entered the room. It was wearing a dinner jacket and smoking a pipe.

"Well?" said the nephew.

"I don't know who it is. Hang on, I'm thinking."

Scrooge listened to all this with interest. "I'm enjoying this game. I can't work it out either. Do you know who they are talking about?"

The Ghost of Christmas Present looked at Scrooge, his mouth smeared with toffee and chocolate.

Anthony Lund

"You're a disgrace," Scrooge told him. "Regardless, do you know the answer?"

"I thought you were meant to be intelligent."

"I matched Carol Vorderman in my last MENSA test."

"I want the results checking."

"Look, just because I'm clever it doesn't mean I'm good at games like this. I'm a bit out of practice with these things."

"Scrooge," the Spirit said, withdrawing a large slab of spice cake from his robe. "If he wasn't unconscious, even Jimmy McThickhead-O'Donnell would know the answer to this one. Would you like a clue?"

"That's very generous."

"It's you."

"I'm not generous. You wouldn't be here if I was."

"I'm really beginning to wish I wasn't here. I meant the answer is you."

Scrooge remained quiet a short moment while he pondered this. "That's really not nice."

"Well it's the truth."

"You tell me you're going to give me a clue then come out and tell me the answer. Where's the fun in that?"

The Spirit contemplated taking out the Big Red Book again, but decided to hold back. He was only halfway through a chunk of Christmas cake and didn't want to stop for some unplanned violence.

"What was the answer I just told you?' the Spirit asked.

A Christmas Carol – Retold

"You."

"No. You, not me."

"I didn't say you. You said you, and I said you meaning me."

"What time is it, Mr Scrooge?"

"I don't know. Your buddy nicked my watch." Scrooge looked around and spotted the clock on the mantelpiece. He found another one that was striped. "It's four minutes to two and forty-five seconds. Forty-six. Forty-seven."

"Ok I get the idea. That means it's almost time for me to leave you...thank god."

"You make it sound like you're glad to be going."

"Well you're not the greatest person to spend time with. You're moody, peculiarly thick in some respects, miserable and inconsiderate of others."

"Thank you."

"It wasn't a compliment, Scrooge. Now take hold of my robe one last time."

Scrooge knew the routine by now and without a word took hold of the Spirit's robe. Soon they were travelling once more, by houses where merriment was being made, homes that were being filled with joyous laughter and the occasional bedroom where it was best not to linger for fear of being hit by an ecstatically far flung limb. The Spirit visited the beds of the sick and his presence lifted their own spirits, he blessed many,

Anthony Lund

offered prayers to other and stopped frequently to nibble on whatever food passed his chubby hands.

Although Vodka had told Scrooge his time was growing short they seemed to spend much time going from scene to scene, until finally they stood in an old country lane and Scrooge looked upon the Spirit as though he had never laid eyes on him before.

The Spirit had inexplicably aged during their time together. His hair was grey, as was his beard. Even his robe seemed to have waned although the big red book remained as vibrant and as painful looking as ever.

"You look like shit," Scrooge said.

"You've looked better yourself," Vodka replied while removing bits of food from between his teeth.

"So is that it? You just live for this long?"

"I'm not technically alive, Scrooge. Do try and keep up. My time is short here though, although one of my brothers will always be there to take up the role. At midnight I will be gone."

"Midnight? Why's it always happen at midnight?"

Vodka smiled. "It adds to the effect. You know; black night, creeping fog the distant chime of the church —"

BONG!

"Holy shit!" Scrooge cried. "You could have warned me you'd stopped right under the bell tower.

BONG!

"Sorry, must have slipped my mind."

99

A Christmas Carol – Retold

"Well it's almost time for me to go," Vodka said rising to his feet.

BONG!

"Wait!" Scrooge said. "There is something sticking out of your robe."

The Spirit looked down. "Bugger," he said, tucking it back in.

BONG!

"No I didn't mean that!" Scrooge said. "That's been hanging out all night. I meant that!"

The ghost looked further down. From the bottom of his robes poked what appeared to be four feet, none of which belonged to him.

The ghost pulled open his robes to reveal two skeletally thin children. There was one boy and one girl, both wretched and starved, both matted with dirt and smelling like something in desperate need of a burst of Glade freshness. They wore rags and had chunks of hair missing. Their eyes bulged in their sockets and their lips were cracked and dry. All in all they were never going to win any modelling contracts…then again…they did have the figure for it.

Scrooge looked at the children aghast. He had never seen anything so pitiful, and for the first time this night he was pleased he had not eaten.

BONG!

"Do these belong to you?" Scrooge asked.

Anthony Lund

"Yes I bought them at the Supermarket on the way to meet you," Vodka said.

"What?!"

BONG!

"Of course they aren't mine! They belong to the likes of you. They belong to the human race. The boy is Ignorance and the girl is Want."

"Their parents should be shot. What kind of girl has a name like Want? I can just see the way the kids at school will treat her."

"These are the children of Doom," Vodka said.

BONG!

"Dr Doom? Well that explains something I guess."

"No, the Doom of mankind. Beware these two on your journey through life or they will destroy everything you hold true. They will slaughter hope, tear out the guts of peace and use them as jewellery, climb inside the rotting, blood-stained, maggot infected– "

BONG!

"Whoa, whoa whoa!" Scrooge burst in. "I get the picture! This isn't an Italian zombie horror story you know!"

"Sorry, I sometimes get carried away."

"Bloody right you do. Anyway, is there nowhere for these two to go?"

"What? Prisons and workhouses? That's where you would put them wouldn't you?"

BONG!

"I said that didn't I?" Scrooge said, wincing.

"Yes you did," the Spirit said, closing his robe around the children and reaching into his pocket to extract a packet of biscuits. "You're quite inconsiderate sometimes."

"Me?" Scrooge asked incredulously. "How can you call me inconsiderate when I've had to spend most of the time I've been with you in the freezing snow, having my feet burned and being forced to starve while you act like you're re-enacting Caesar's Banquet?"

BONG!

"I'm a growing boy."

"You could have grown a school of them on the amount you've eaten. You could have even given some to those poor wretches in there!"

"You're starting to think about others for once. Good, good. Now as much as I would like to remain here and trade insults with you all night, you have another appointment and you mustn't be late for this one. Hold this."

BONG!

The ghost passed Scrooge the packet of biscuits. Scrooge, against all better judgement, immediately pulled one out and moved it to his mouth, determined to get something out of the night.

Anthony Lund

The Big Red Book swung around and before Scrooge could react it knocked the biscuit from his hand, and on the backswing knocked him off his feet.

"Ebenezer Scrooge," the Ghost of Christmas Present said. "This is your death."

BONG!

Stave IV

Whiskey – The Sobering Spirit.

Scrooge awakened on his bedroom floor.

He felt like he had been hit by a train...one in the shape a Big Red Book.

He sat up. His head throbbed, his body ached and his trousers were still wet from the earlier incident with the plate of jelly. It sounded like the aftermath of a Stag night.

Scrooge looked around the bedroom. The place was clean at least, although he did notice a few crumbs here and there. He went to stand up and thumped against the underside of the Ghost's banquet table.

"He could have left food, but instead he leaves the table! Bah! Black jacks!"

Scrooge crawled out into the open and lifted himself up using his enemy, the table, for support.

Suddenly and without warning, the table vanished and Scrooge struck the floor with a squelch. The jelly had not disappeared. Marley had failed to tell him how bad for his health his visitors were going to be. When the night was over Scrooge was going to exhume his partner's body and pick as many bones as he could.

"Ok,' Scrooge said, picking himself up again. "Let's get this over with. Do your worst."

A dark shadow fell over him. It hit his bedside table and crumpled in a heap.

"Sorry about that," Scrooge said. "You should watch where you're walking."

The dark figure slowly rose to its feet. Scrooge took the rose and put it in a vase.

The figure wore a black robe. It had just come out of the shower. All Scrooge could see of a body were the hands. They were made of nothing but bone.

"You haven't been hanging around with the Ghost of Christmas Present have you?" Scrooge asked.

The Spirit didn't reply.

"Why do I get the feeling this is going to be bad? You must be Whiskey, right?"

The Spirit nodded.

"Whiskey always was my least favourite spirit. So far I've had the thief, the glutton and now I have the happy reaper."

The Spirit remained silent.

Anthony Lund

"Come on then. If that's the small talk out of the way lets get into the heavy stuff."

The Spirit snapped its fingers. Two bits of broken bone dropped to the floor.

"Did you plan to do that?" Scrooge asked. "Never mind. I'm sure they'll grow back. Unlike my thumbs. You're going to show me the future right?"

The Spirit, in an unexpected, completely out of character move, did not speak but just nodded.

"You know you're scaring the shit out of me right now?"

The Spirit nodded.

"And I will listen to your words... erm... visions and take them all on board."

The Spirit nodded.

"Did I mention that you're scaring the shit out of me?"

The Spirit – all together now – nodded.

"Ok, ok, lead on," Scrooge said.

Whiskey turned slowly and silently away, an eerie move that would have not been out of place in a Japanese horror movie. As frightened as he was, Scrooge knew he had to follow. The Spirit drifted away and Scrooge followed in its wake.

In the blink of an eye, the flick of a wrist and the twist of a nipple, Scrooge found himself once more in the snow covered streets of the city.

"Why outside again?" Scrooge complained. "Don't you know I'm damp with jelly? I'll catch my death out here!"

A Christmas Carol – Retold

The number Death bus passed by. Scrooge missed it.

The Spirit remained a burning beacon of joy – someone had just forgotten to light it. It raised a hand to point Scrooge in the direction he should be looking. Scrooge was beginning to long for the irritating banter of the other Spirits.

The Ghost was pointing to a group of men standing a short distance away. Scrooge walked over to the group, sticking his head in the only gap he could find in the circle. He prayed the man had not eaten Indian the night before.

The conversation seemed to revolve around death although whose death Scrooge could not tell. He hated walking in on a conversation half way through. He listened.

"So, anyone know what happened to the money?" one said.

"Don't know but I heard there was a lot of it," said another.

"How much?"

"It had three pound signs in front of it."

"Well he couldn't take it with him, could it?"

"I heard that heaven was branching out. Have you not seen their new bank on the high street? The bank that likes to take it with you."

"He won't have gone to heaven though. He'll have gone on the express train south."

"Where? Torquay?"

"No I mean the hot place."

Anthony Lund

"Bournemouth? Lucky bugger."

"You're a fool, Nobby."

"Is that higher ranking than a numpty? I've been at numpty level for a while now."

Scrooge carefully backed out from between Nobby's legs. He wasn't sure about the whereabouts of the unfortunate deceased but the conversation was certainly dragging the bottom of the sense barrel.

"Well that was informative," Scrooge said to Whiskey. "I would ask you to tell me the point but I can guess the response I'd get."

The Spirit said nothing.

"Exactly," Scrooge said. "So where do we go next? To watch someone washing windows?"

The Spirit raised a finger and pointed. Scrooge followed the direction of the finger and suddenly noticed they were no longer in the city. They were now in a dark place on the edge of the town that Scrooge had never been before. The buildings were ugly, the people staggering about were drunk, swearing at each other and wearing very few clothes. The streets stank of crime, dirt, sex and devilry. Scrooge wondered what had stopped him coming here before.

Scrooge's eyes fell upon what the Spirit wanted him to see. It was a rundown excuse for a building on the other side of the road.

"It looks like a shop," Scrooge said.

111

A sign above it read, "Shop."

Whiskey applauded Scrooge's powers of observation then bent to pick up its hands which had fallen off. Scrooge went inside while the Spirit put itself together.

The shop was full of what looked like used upholstery.

"Are we looking for anything in particular, Dear," Scrooge said. "I thought flowers might go well with the décor but I think it might clash with your robe."

Whiskey slapped Scrooge across the face. It was like being struck with a handful of stale breadsticks.

"Is there a body I can complain to about brutality? A dead body I'm presuming."

The Spirit replied by pointing towards the back of the room. There a woman sat behind a desk that was buried under what appeared to be a week of dirty washing. Beside her were a handful of people Scrooge did not know. As they were all carrying bed sheets and curtains that looked vaguely familiar he wondered whether he should be able to say he knew them.

"So what have you got there, Bill?" the woman asked one of the men.

"I don't have the bill, I didn't pay for them."

"I should say not. What kind of scavengers pay for what they scavenge?"

"I think they're called London Market Traders these days."

Anthony Lund

"Well that's not us then," the woman said, satisfied at her conclusion. "So anyway what do you have there?"

"A flock of sheep."

"That's funny it looks like curtains to me."

"Of course it's curtains, you silly old bat," Bill said. "I've already dropped the sheep at the butchers."

Bill dumped the heap of fabric on the table. It was hard to tell where one item ended and the others started. Scrooge realised that he was only assuming there was desk somewhere under the mess, although he was coming to realise that it may not be so.

"Nice curtains," Scrooge said. "I've got some just like them."

The woman pawed at the curtains. Scrooge was almost certain she was just trying to clean some dirt off her hands. She turned them over, folded them, turned them again, tossed them in the air and folded them one last time.

"There," she said. "I told them you could do origami with more than just paper."

"So what are they worth," Bill asked.

"Normal or as a goose?"

"Normal."

"Six bob."

"My name is Bill."

"I don't care what your name is. It's still six bob."

"I'll take it." Bill pulled a wad of cash out of his pocket, paid the woman and left with the curtains.

"Hang on a minute," Scrooge said. "Isn't she meant to pay him for them and then take them off him?"

The Spirit nodded in reply.

"I wonder if she would consider working for me."

Scrooge watched as the next person deposited a load on the heap.

"Couldn't you have waited, Alice?" the woman said. "I've got to get a cloth to clean that up now."

"Sorry. I've got some bed sheets if you want to use them."

"No, they'll be dirty enough. From what I heard he was too mean to buy any washing powder so god knows how long he's been lying in them."

"The same length as when he was standing up. He didn't grow at night."

"Good point. How long have you had them?"

"Well they're straight from his bed, so they're still a bit warm and damp."

The woman cackled. "Really? Well I can pay you extra for that. Anything warm and damp gets snapped up straight away."

"I should have taken his underwear."

"Let's not go too far now, Alice. I have to draw the line somewhere."

Anthony Lund

"I draw my line on a piece of paper then I can take it with
me."

"Good idea, girl. I might try that."

Scrooge watched the scene in fascination. This was an
achievement as the village of Fascination was ten miles north.

"Who is the poor man they are talking about? Have they
really been and taken his belongings to sell for their own gain?
That is so wickedly ruthless. Do you have a pen so I can take
notes?"

The Spirit picked Scrooge up by his collar and threw him
out of the door into the street. Scrooge spat out a mouthful of
snow and with effort stood up.

"I want to claim damages," he complained. "If you would
talk to me it would be a lot easier. It would be a lot less painful
too. You're not on a sponsored silence are you?"

Whiskey's only response was to snap his fingers again.

Scrooge felt something pressing against his back.
Turning around he found a long bed behind him.

They were indoors, standing by a stark bed on which lay
a body covered by a single dirty-white sheet. Scrooge did not
think he was going to be pleased with any outcome from this
scene.

Whiskey pointed to sheet covering the face of the dead.

"That's just sick!" Scrooge said. "Aren't there laws
against this kind of thing? You know, fiddling with the dead and
all that? They lock people up for less."

The Spirit did nothing but point.

Scrooge was now beyond being scared. He was slowly ticking over into the territory of terrified. He wanted to be gone from this bedside. It was lonely, dark, morbid, there was no hint of sex, drugs or alcohol...although...

"Thumbs!" Scrooge hissed with glee. "He won't be needing his thumbs!"

Scrooge moved towards the body, his mind set on the purpose of robbing the dead body of the digits it would no longer need, but as he moved the sheet, the bed and its occupant vanished. Scrooge was left with an empty hand and the fading impression that the hand beneath the sheet had been as void of thumbs as his own hands. Odd.

The room around them became brighter and transformed before Scrooge's eyes into a small but comfortable kitchen. A young woman and her daughter sat at the table, seemingly waiting for something.

"Who are they waiting f –"

The door Scrooge had failed to notice swung inwards and knocked him to the floor.

"Sweet Caroline!" shouted the man rushing into the room. "Good days never seemed so close! He's dead, he's dead, he's dead! Our problems are over and our debts are gone!"

"Are you sure, Darling? He's really dead? Oh, how wonderful!"

Scrooge staggered up from the floor.

Anthony Lund

"What is it with you ghosts and your teleportational-ismatroic whatnot jobs or whatever it is? No one can see me or hear me but they can all injure me! And who is this poor bugger everyone is so happy to see dead? Is there anyone who is sorry for him?"

Whiskey spoke not a word, which was just what Scrooge had come to expect.

"This is not how it's meant to be. People should be sorry when someone dies, they should mourn their loss and feel compassion towards their dead. Show me the compassion!"

Whiskey lifted his robe.

"I said the compassion, not the competition! Anyway Vodka beats you by a foot...four feet actually."

When Whiskey dropped his robe, Scrooge found they were once again in the street. The Spirit pointed to the building before them. This one Scrooge recognised from earlier in the night.

"Bob Cratchit's house again? It's only an hour since I was last here. I'm not an amnesiac, you know. Plus my feet are still sore off the last time."

The bony finger continued to point.

"Have you ever thought of a career directing traffic? Or as a signpost?"

The Spirit did not move.

"How about as one of those living statues?" The skeletal hand began to ball into a fist. "Ok, I'm going in. I'm going in. Don't hit me again."

Scrooge entered the Cratchit house, making sure to avoid the area of his last visit. He emerged next to the sink.

The house was somehow different to the last time Scrooge had been. It was as though it was a different house.

He felt a tap on his shoulder. He turned it off. He hated to hear the sound of dripping.

Another tap came, this time from a bony finger. He turned around. The Ghost of Christmas Yet To Come jerked a thumb to the left. Scrooge followed the line of indication to see a family picture hanging on the wall. It wasn't the Cratchits. He was in the wrong house.

Scrooge followed the Ghost back into the dark, snowy street.

The Ghost pointed to an identical house next door.

"You sent me into the wrong house? Are you sure you're qualified for this job?"

The Spirit shrugged and continued to point.

"If this one isn't right, then I want a replacement ghost. I'm not having some rookie. I'm a special case, in need of a stern hand."

The ghost gave him a stern hand across the face.

"Oww."

Anthony Lund

Scrooge walked into the Cratchit house, rubbing his face. He was going to look like he'd been mugged in the morning. He made a mental note to remember to put in a mugging claim as soon as the bruises started to show.

The Cratchit house was dimly lit. The family were sitting around the dinner table very much as they had been the last time he had seen them. The food was gone. And the chair that had contained Tiny Tim was empty as was that in which Bob had been seated.

He was about to ask the Spirit where they were, and was half way through realising how pointless that would be when the door to the house opened and Bob walked in dusting a light covering of snow from his head.

"Bob!" Mrs Cratchit said. "How many times have I told you not to brush your dandruff all over the floor?"

"Sorry, dear," Bob said. "You know how bad it gets. Everyone's beginning to think that's snow outside."

Scrooge gagged. He'd wondered why it had tasted of Head and Shoulders.

"So how was church?" Mrs Cratchit asked.

"Same as always. It tends to seem a little darker in there than it used to."

"That'll be those energy saving light bulbs they put in. They never seem as bright as normal ones."

"It always seems like I've forgotten something."

"You did. You've got no shoes on."

119

"I thought my feet seemed cold."

"It's such a shame that Tim can't be here still," Mrs Cratchit sighed, a tear in her eye. "He did love going to that church. He loved to bless everyone. He was so caring and full of love for everyone and everything."

"I know," said Bob. "Are you sure he wasn't adopted?"

"No he wasn't."

"Just checking."

"Where's his crutch?"

Bob looked at the fireplace.

Mrs Cratchit looked sadly at the fire. "Oh yes. There it is."

Bob lifted the crutch off the bracket over the mantelpiece. "I still prefer the Fender in there instead."

"Yes it's a shame we had to use it for firewood."

"We what?!"

"Sorry," Mrs Cratchit said. "I did ask you and you agreed."

"When?"

"I asked you in bed last night."

"No you didn't!"

"You were asleep. I asked you could we use your guitar for firewood, I elbowed you in the ribs and you grunted in affirmation."

"How do you know it was in affirmation?"

"I got hold of your head and nodded it to be certain."

Anthony Lund

Bob looked crestfallen. "Oh, well in that case I must have agreed," he said, bending down to pick up his crest.

Scrooge turned away from the family to look at the Spirit. "I thought I was miserable and all, but you...you...how can you show me this? That man has just had his guitar burned! That's the cruellest twist of fate I can imagine."

The Ghost pulled a piece of card from its robe. He had obviously pre-empted Scrooge's response. On it was written, "WHAT ABOUT THE LOSS OF THEIR SON?"

"That is terrible," Scrooge said. "All this time you've been pointing and gesturing at me and you had card and a pen all along? You're despicable."

"DON'T BE SMART," the next card read.

"Sorry. Where did they lose him? Hasn't someone handed him in?"

"I FEEL A MOMENT OF VIOLENCE APPROACHING."

"Does that mean I'll feel it shortly?"

"YES."

"Which direction is it coming from? I'll try to duck."

The Spirit hit Scrooge with an uppercut then turned over the piece of card. "BETTER LUCK NEXT TIME."

Scrooge lay on his back and rubbed his jaw. It was still attached to his face. That was always a bonus.

He sat up and found himself in a graveyard. This was clever as he had not known he was lost there.

A Christmas Carol – Retold

It was dark. It was eerie. The grass needed cutting and the tree branch poking him in the ear was becoming irritating.

He looked around for the Spirit. The branch poked him in the eye.

"Bugger," he said.

He turned the other way and found Whiskey standing silently - no surprise there - holding another piece of card.

"MIND THE BRANCHES."

"Thanks. A little late in the day, but I can feel the sentiment. My eye can feel the branch."

Scrooge got to his feet. Something wasn't right. He looked down.

"Where's my trousers?"

"LOST IN TRANSIT."

"I haven't been to Transit. I haven't been any further than Southampton!"

"DON'T SWEAT. WE'RE NEARLY DONE HERE. YOU'LL SURVIVE."

"I'll be adding it to my compensation claim."

"GOOD LUCK."

"So what joy am I going to take from this place?"

The Spirit pointed to something behind Scrooge. He turned around and found a gravestone there. Not unusual in a graveyard.

The stone was coated in white and Scrooge could not read the name.

Anthony Lund

"Bob Cratchit hasn't been here has he?"

"NO. IT'S SNOW."

"Good. What's so special about this one?"

The ghost pointed.

"Why am I getting a bad feeling about this?"

"I HAVE NO IDEA WHAT YOU MEAN."

"Of course you don't. How many years have you been in this job?"

The finger pointed again.

"Ok. Ok. Just tell me, can these things be changed?"

"NO."

"No? That's not right!"

The Spirit looked at the card then flipped it over.

"YES."

"That's better. The whole thing would have been a bit of a waste of everyone's time otherwise."

The Spirit pointed to the grave again.

Scrooge leaned forward and wiped away the snow.

"'Jimmy McThickhead O'Donnell'," he read. "'Died tragically by Guinness bottle.' What?"

Scrooge looked at the Spirit who managed to look embarrassed. He pulled a plan of the graveyard out of his robe, ran his finger over it then pointed to another stone.

"It's really not your night is it?" Scrooge asked approaching the other stone.

Once again he wiped away the frost.

123

A Christmas Carol – Retold

EBENEZER SCROOGE, it read.

"Well ain't that a kick in the head?"

"IT IS NOT TOO LATE TO CHANGE THIS."

"Good. I don't like the design of the stone at all. Too much decoration. I want something simple."

"CHANGE YOUR WAYS, EBENEZER."

The Spirit turned away and began to walk across the graveyard. Scrooge got to his feet, attached them to his legs and went after the Spirit.

"Wait. You can't leave me here. I want to ask you about my thumbs!"

The Spirit continued walking.

Scrooge ran after the Ghost, falling to his knees beside it and grasping a handful of its robe.

"I will change, Spirit! I will, I promise. I am not the same man I was before and I am only a shadow of the man I intend to become."

Whiskey handed down a card. "YOU SOUND A LITTLE CONFUSED."

"No I have never able to see so clear!" Scrooge said. "I will remember all the Spirits –mainly through scars and bruises – and the lessons they have taught me."

Whiskey shook off Scrooge's grip and once more walked away into the rising mist.

"Spirit! Don't leave me."

Anthony Lund

A piece of card flew over the ghost's shoulder as he vanished. Scrooge caught it with his face. He pulled it out and read it.

"A RELATIONSHIP JUST WOULDN'T WORK. WE HAVE TOO MANY DIFFERENCES."

Scrooge looked up from the card and screamed at the sight of a haggard face before him leering out of the mist.

Stave V

Hangover – The Morning After.

The face in the mist screamed back at Scrooge.

The mirror cracked under the pressure.

Scrooge closed his mouth. Six images in front of him did the same. He was home, in his bathroom with the hot water tap running.

He looked out into the bedroom. The bed was not occupied by the body of his own corpse, his bed sheets had not been removed and the curtains still hung from their rails

Outside it was daylight but what day Scrooge could not tell. It seemed that he had been walking with the three Spirits for more time than he could comprehend. He moved over to the window and flung it open. He hung out and called down to a young woman.

"What day is it today?"

The woman looked up. "You dirty old man!"

Scrooge was taken aback. Then he noticed he had no clothes on. He quickly pulled the window closed and retreated into his bedroom. A moment later he returned full dressed.

This time a young boy was passing.

"You boy," he shouted. "What day is it?"

"Wednesday."

"Which Wednesday?"

"The same one it is every week. Comes between Tuesday and Thursday."

"Ok. What day is tomorrow?"

"Thursday."

"If I give you some money will you give me the answers I want?"

"If you tell me the answers as well."

"Deal. I'll ask the question and I want you to answer Christmas Day."

"Ok."

"What day is it today?"

"Christmas day," the boy said with a grin, holding his hand out for payment.

"How do I know you're not lying?"

"Because you told me the answer."

"True."

Scrooge threw a handful of coins from his window. They hit the boy in the face.

Anthony Lund

"Gee thanks Mister," the boy said. "You didn't say you were going to give me a black eye for free."

"Take it as a bonus. If you do what I ask then I'll give you another one."

"Great," said the boy. "It'll save me having to wear make-up for my panda costume in the school play."

"Ok. Here's what I want."

*

A short time later, Scrooge bounded out of his front door. The smell of Christmas was in the air – someone was burning the turkey.

The streets were full of people, the pubs were full of people, the roads were full of people, and everyone's houses were full of burglars making the most of them all being empty. Scrooge trotted along the path, shouting Merry Christmas to everyone who would listen and chasing those who would not until they agreed to.

Turning a corner, Scrooge came face to face with two familiar faces. They belonged to the Suspicious Charity collectors.

"Good Christmas morning to you," Scrooge bellowed, blowing the two men's faces inside out. "How delightful it is to see you again!"

"Ah, yes, Mr Scrooge, isn't it?" one of the men ventured.

131

"That's my name indeed. Say it again."

"Mr Scrooge."

"One more time."

"Mr Scrooge."

"Let me hear you say it with your heart!"

"Mr Scrooge." The two men said in unison.

"Good good. Now I believe when you came to me yesterday you were discussing gathering money for a charity supporting all the bastards in the world. I would like to give you something for them."

Scrooge hit one of the men with his cane.

"Give each of them one of those and tell them to get a proper job! Now if you would like to discuss setting up a better charity, such as one supporting dwarves who cannot reach supermarket shelves or saving endangered animals in Botswana, then I would be happy to give you an initial donation of –"

Scrooge pulled the two men close to him. Their heads knocked together and one of the men collapsed holding his eye. Scrooge whispered a sum of money in the other collector's ear. The second collector collapsed with shock.

"Come and see me when you have both pulled yourselves together!" Scrooge said, skipping away down the road. "Good day you!"

Soon Scrooge arrived at his nephew's house. After a moment of doubt he knocked on the door.

Anthony Lund

A very pretty young girl opened it. Scrooge forced himself not to drool and remembered why he had finally taken the plunge to knock at the door.

"Excuse-me-but-my-nephew-lives-here-and-i've-come-to-see-him-but-first-i-really-have-to-use-the-toilet."

Scrooge was halfway along the hall by the time the rapid-fire sentence had left off his lips. When he return, relieved, his nephew and family were waiting for him.

"Uncle Scrooge," his nephew said. "This is a bit of a surprise."

"Well I couldn't stand the thought of all that turkey lying around until Easter so thought I would come and help you eat some of it."

"Get in!" Scrooge's nephew bellowed. "I told you he would come around. Now let me just get the book and you can all pay up now. You see it is always best to bet against the odds!"

Scrooge remembered he had an appointment to keep with his clerk. He made his apologies and promised his nephew that he would return later in the day for food, drink and a merry old time playing blind-man's buff.

A short time later, Scrooge arrived at Bob Cratchit's door. He straightened up his overcoat and knocked with his cane as someone had stolen the knocker.

Bob opened the door. "Mister Scrooge! This is a surprise."

"Really? I knew it was planned," Scrooge said, pushing past Bob.

"Do come in," said Bob. "Take a seat."

"I'll stand."

"Well we don't normally allow people to stand on the furniture but if you really want to."

Scrooge found the Cratchit family gathered around the table. They had not begun to prepare their dinner.

"You know that I've let you have today off, Bob?" Scrooge said.

"Yes, Mister Scrooge."

"Well I think I was wrong."

There was a clattering of metal from the table. Mrs Cratchit stood up with a frying pan in her hand.

"I knew he'd want you to work, Bob. It's not going to happen."

Mrs Cratchit ran at Scrooge, the frying pan swinging about her head like a club. She let out a yell that rattled the cutlery.

Scrooge stepped to one side, allowing her to storm past him. He winced as the frying pan connected with Bob's head. He wondered if the Spirits had meant to teach him dodge manoeuvres.

Scrooge waited until Bob regained consciousness then continued.

"Like I said, I think I was wrong…"

Anthony Lund

Bob held his wife back.

"…I should have told you to take the rest of the week off."

There was a thud as Bob's jaw hit the floor. At the table Tiny Tim turned around.

"Fuc–" was as far as he got before a raw sprout found its way into his mouth.

"And," Scrooge said. "I want to give you a raise. I've had your chair legs extended by three inches and bought you a pair of shoes with heels."

Bob's head fell off to join his jaw. He felt the floor by his feet until he found his head and put it back on.

"Oh," said Scrooge. "And I want to make you my partner."

"I'm already married, Mister Scrooge," Bob said.

"In the business."

"Ah."

"So what do you say?"

"Thank you, Mister Scrooge."

"I meant do you accept the offer."

"Yes."

There was a knock at the door;it was carrying a giant goose.

"Now, Bob," said Scrooge. "I know you've wanted this for a long time. So I decided–"

135

A Christmas Carol – Retold

Scrooge was flattened by the Cratchit family as they charged at the goose. He picked himself up and dusted himself off.

"There's no need to rush. There's plenty for–"

Scrooge hit the floor again as the family returned indoors with the goose carried over their heads like a sacrificial lamb for the gods.

"Bah! Humbug!" Scrooge said.

There was another knock at the door. It was a popular door. Scrooge pulled himself up on the handle and opened it. On the step stood a short man with glasses, a clip board and a calculator.

"Mr Scrooge?" he asked.

"Yes."

"I'm from the Bah Humbug Corporation. You owe us five pounds for use of a copyrighted phrase of ours."

"That was quick. I was expecting an invoice with a Speak Now Pay Later option. Do they really make you work on Christmas Day?"

"It's our busiest time. We don't get time off at Christmas. Can you pay up now, I have another appointment?"

Scrooge handed over the money. "Does your boss have a partner?"

"No, but he has been to a few singles nights recently."

"In the business sense."

Anthony Lund

"No, in the personal sense. I don't think they do singles nights for business purposes."

Scrooge resisted the urge to slap the man. "Does he have a business partner?"

"Ah, sadly no. He died a few years ago."

Scrooge nodded. "He might be about to see him again. Keep your nose clean and you may be in line for a promotion soon."

"Do you have a crystal ball?"

"No, they looked ordinary when I got dressed this morning. Just take my word for it."

"Well I don't intend to check them."

"I meant about the promotion."

"Oh, ok. Good day, Mr Scrooge."

Scrooge closed the door and turned to the Cratchit family sitting around the table. In front of them was the almighty sparkling carcass of the goose.

"That's got to be some kind of record," Scrooge said.

"No it's a CD playing in the living room," Bob said.

"Well I'm sure you'll all be blessed with indigestion later in the day. I'll see you at work next week, Bob. If you call in sick though I won't be best pleased."

"Don't worry, Mr Scrooge. I won't."

"Well in that case, I have other people to see."

"Can I just ask, Mr Scrooge? Why are you being so nice?"

"It's the Spirits. They made me see things differently."

"Things blurry are they?"

"No. They're much clearer than they were before."

"I'd like to try it sometime."

"Well if your wife hits you with that frying pan a few more times then you'll be halfway there."

"Thanks for the advice, Mr Scrooge, and Merry Christmas. God bless us."

The room waited in silence. Everyone looked at Tiny Tim, who was poking the hump of his stomach.

"Tim," Bob said. "It's your line."

"It's just a crease from the way I've been sitting."

"I meant the God bless us line."

"Oh right. God bless us every one. You cun – errrrrp!"

The belch blew the goose carcass off the table. It danced on the wind, performed the Austrian Waltz with Mrs Cratchit, and came to rest against the wall.

"Pardon me." Tim said with a smile.

"And on that note, it was a C sharp I think, I'll leave you to enjoy Christmas."

With that Scrooge headed off to fulfil his promise to his nephew.

From that day on Scrooge was a changed man, starting with his underwear. He created his own charity, Thumbs 4 U, and later he built up a secondary business selling stolen door knockers.

Anthony Lund

Tiny Tim did not die, although he did continue to shout out random curses at inappropriate times. At the age of thirty-two he became a member of parliament where his outbursts were welcomed with open ears, and a few years later he was given the position of Minister for Profanity, something that the country had been lacking a long while. The people of Profanity were delighted to finally have their own minister.

After a bout of food poisoning from eating uncooked goose, the Cratchit family lived their lives in new found wealth. They moved to a new house, installed satellite TV and sent their children off to stage school.

The predictions made to Scrooge by the Spirits still came to pass, just a little later than planned thanks to the changes Scrooge made to his life and the lives around him; he changed their underwear too. The delays in the predictions' ETA did play slight havoc in Fate's diary causing Her no end of appointment changes, although it did mean that lives were happier for it as they were not dead.

The Spirits themselves found other work when they discovered their current vocations weren't going anywhere other than Christmas Past, Christmas Present and Christmas Yet To Come. Gin found employment as a watch seller on Heaven's South Pier, Vodka, with his debonair looks and greying hair, took up the position of Head Chef in Hell's Kitchen, and Whiskey successfully completed a sign language course to help with his communication skills. Learning to speak would have perhaps been simpler.

Scrooge never saw Jacob Marley again and never received the invoice Marley had promised him. He also never found out what had happened to his trousers but it was something he had to live with.

In the end, Scrooge felt that for the price he had paid his deal was a good one. People offered him meals, helped him to decorate and brought him gifts. He was spending less now than he did before. It had all worked out for the best it seemed.

Scrooge came to believe that allowing Christmas to enter his life was the best decision he had made since going to visit Dirty Carrie's and spending an hour in the company of Madame Lucia. Ah, the memories.

And as we leave our story, the words of Tiny Tim ring in our ears forever more. God bless us, every one. You country bumpkins!

The End.

Author's Note

As always with anything I touch, there is a story

behind the writing of this book. There are some people who like to know which fruit the juices of creativity are squeezed from, and just as many who would rather have their own extremities squeezed than listen to an author dribbling into his own ego over how he created an earth-shattering masterpiece.

Well, this is where you decide which camp you're in, although I should say that I lost my ego a long time ago and as yet it has not been found. I have my suspicions that it fled the country and is now working in the White House as a direct advisor to the President – come on, he does say some funny things; there must be some kind of comedian behind it.

Anyway, digressions and indigestion aside, and purely for those who are interested in this kind of thing, here is the story behind A Christmas Carol Retold.

It began very simply. Everything I write tends to begin that way but then something happens and it all becomes so much more complicated.

I was working one August Bank Holiday, bored to the point of wondering if it was possible for your brain to resign from its job through lack of prospects, and decided that I would write an article for our company newsletter. Until then I had tried to write humorous stories on a number of occasions but they tended to fall flat. People always tell me that I am a funny person (I think it's a compliment), but that only applies when I have someone to play off. I react to what other people say and do to get the laughs. Working with fictional characters on a page is a whole different ball game.

Despite my belief that I could be creating something that would be boring, dull and nothing more than an outpouring of senseless drivel, I pressed on a wrote a short piece entitled "August Bank Holiday Apocalypse." I wasn't being dramatic at all.

The article was written, ending up as something that described images not too dissimilar to the cartoons from Monty Python's Flying Circus, or the kind of illustrations used in political cartoons, and was submitted. That month it appeared in the Newsletter and I was dragged into a meeting for a light bollocking.

It seems that what I had written had touched a nerve in that under the humour was a subtext that working in a bank's call centre on a Bank Holiday was ludicrous, a waste of time and not something that people should volunteer for. I didn't even know I had given the piece a

Anthony Lund

subtext, but reading it back later I did see that it was more of a sharp-tongued satire than slapstick comedy.

The outcome of our little meeting was that they liked what I had written, thought it was very well done and wanted me to do a regular article…although they did say they wanted to be able to review the piece before it was published. I was happy to do that and for the next year I submitted monthly articles giving my slant on the events happening around the centre. On a couple of occasions I veered away from the witty commentary to create short pieces of fiction involving lost diaries travelling on great expeditions, staff members becoming roving reporters and Birthday Buffets being eaten by hordes of marauding hooligans. Suddenly I was writing humour without any effort. A 1000 word article was taking me about thirty minutes to write and, with only minor editing for spelling errors and typos, it was usually the first draft that went out.

A year later I moved departments and decided it was time to create something new for the newsletter. I ended what was now known as "The News at 10 and A Half" on its first anniversary, and introduced its replacement – Tales From The Back Side.

The new article was meant to push my boundaries, and give me a bigger challenge – to write a brand new piece of fiction every month.

I began with a look at Greek Goddess Athena, followed by pieces on the origins of Halloween and the story of Guy Fawkes. Then came the article that turned everything on its head.

147

A Christmas Carol – Retold

I needed to write something for the Christmas newsletter and had the idea of parodying Dickens' A Christmas Carol. Up until then, the articles had been about 1000 words long and certainly no longer than 1500. I began writing with the intention of keeping it to that length, but the story conspired against me and soon I had 4000 words and still more than half of the story to go. After some bargaining I was granted space on the company's intranet site to post the full story and also wrote a version of The Nativity for the newsletter (which was banned for being too controversial).

At around the same time I decided to set up my own website to post my work for a wider audience to see. www.talesfromthebackside.co.uk was born at that moment, and as well as giving me a platform for the stories I was writing, it also allowed me to go further with them than I could in a company newsletter – on the site I could play by my own rules and no one could ban The Nativity piece.

The version of A Christmas Carol Retold that appeared on the intranet was just under 10,000 words long, contained no swearing and very few near the knuckle jokes. I knew the story could be pushed further so a few months later I returned to the original document and began working through it, extending scenes, adding new ones, deleting jokes that didn't work.

By the time I finished I had discovered more about Dickens' original tale than I knew before and had a final draft two and a half times longer than the previous version. This is that version – the definitive author cut if you like.

Anthony Lund

So that is the story of what led me to take on the work of one of our greatest authors, deconstruct it and lovingly glue it back together into some kind of Frankenstein's Monster. I hope people read it in the way it is meant – a well known, well loved story being looked at in another way. And if you haven't done so already, the I really would suggest you should read the original Dickens version…better still go out and buy a copy and read it every year, just to remind yourself of the true spirit of Christmas.

Take Care.

Anthony Lund
2nd November 2007

www.ingramcontent.com/pod-product-compliance
Lightning Source LLC
Chambersburg PA
CBHW031916160426
42812CB00106B/3009/J